Champagne at Three

The Story of a Trans Mining Engineer

Jill Blee

rainshadow

© 2025 Copyright Jill Blee
ISBN: (paperback) 978-1-7637356-1-3

Published by Jill Blee and Rainshadow books, an imprint of
Clouds of Magellan Press, Melbourne

www.cloudsofmagellanpress.net

All rights reserved. No part of this publication may be reproduced
without permission of the author.

Design: Gordon Thompson
All images supplied by author
Front top left image: Peter Menzel

Contents

Introduction	1
Margie and Barney	10
A Good Catholic Education	17
Career Options	29
Untying the Apron Strings	42
Mount Isa Mines	51
Mia	65
The Mine Manager's Ticket	68
Hatches Creek	76
A Mining Gypsy	84
Becoming Rebecca	98
The Captain	107
Surgery	114
Getting the Paperwork in Order	120
Working for the Big Australian	126
Mining Consultant	135
Mining in Pakistan	142
Life after the Captain	149
Costerfield	155
Broke in Ballarat	159
Coming Home	167
Rescuing Rebecca from Herself	172
All Together in Ballarat	177
Requiem	182
Slow Decline	186

Introduction

As we gathered around the ruins of the Jubilee Mine on the outskirts of Ballarat to scatter Rebecca's ashes and then to drink to her memory at my daughter Emma's house in Golden Point in October 2017, we did what families always do on such occasions – we talked about Rebecca or, more precisely, what we didn't know about Rebecca.

Although most of us present were cousins, some had not heard Rebecca's name mentioned since she became Rebecca in 1973 and knew nothing about the reasons why she had vanished from the conversations families usually have when they come together to celebrate milestones like birthdays and anniversaries. Most of them looked to me for explanations, but though I had spent the previous decade and a half in daily contact with Rebecca, there were large gaps in my knowledge about how she had come to decide that the gender she had been assigned at birth was wrong, or what she had undergone both physically and psychologically to rectify what she believed to be the anomaly of her birth.

As we sipped champagne, Rebecca's drink of choice, I decided to write her biography, a task which would take me the best part of six years. It should have been easy to write about Rebecca's early life, because for the first twenty years of it we lived under the same roof, being raised by the same parents. However, while I could remember some of the more momentous events of our childhood, and I was aware of considerable rivalry between us as we both sought recognition from our parents and teachers, I don't recall us ever confiding in each other.

With our knowledge of, and interest in each other dissipating once we had both left home to embark on our careers, uncovering the rest of Rebecca's story involved tracking down people with whom she had lived and worked over the next 56 years of her life. Some who had known her both as Robert Michael Norton and Rebecca Michelle Norton had themselves passed away and there were others who had nothing worthwhile to say because they could not understand or condone her decision to change gender. Some, particularly old mining engineers with whom she had worked at one time or another, were only too happy to regale me over the telephone with stories that were as much about them as they were about Rebecca.

The information I gleaned from these conversations was enough to construct a rough timeline of Rebecca's working life and it soon became apparent that she had changed employer often, and there were periods of unemployment in the years leading up to her decision to undertake gender affirmation surgery. Afterwards she had to deal with derision from some of her fellow miners as she rebuilt her professional reputation. Eventually, being a self-employed consultant to the mining industry brought her respect and the time she needed to care for the man she always referred to as The Captain. He had befriended her when she was at her lowest ebb, but as he grew increasingly old and fragile over the next decade or so, he exacted repayment for his kindness to her by requiring her constant attention to his needs.

While she was rewarded for her efforts with a generous bequest when the old man died, her life by this time had begun to spin out of control and she seemed unable to plan for a future on her own. For a few years at least, her consulting services were in demand and she became actively involved in the professional associations which provided support and advice to the mining industry, but she made no provision for herself.

Having started the 1990s with a house full of furniture which The Captain's family had accumulated over the years, by the time I was called in to find a place for her to live ten years later, she had hardly anything of note except a battered filing cabinet full of rocks and a folder containing her academic records, her membership certificates of mining engineering organisations and a number of curriculum vitae written towards the end of her working life. Although they were similar in the way they had been constructed, the content varied, presumably to meet the requirements of the intended recipients. Some claimed periods of employment with mining companies which no longer existed, if they ever did, and the lists of referees they contained varied considerably, but they were a starting point for me.

The mining companies Rebecca had referred to were of little help. Those which still existed, or whose history of operations could be readily found such as BHP and Mount Isa Mines, had undergone significant changes over the years and no longer had records of past employees they could access. From newspapers, the internet and industry organisations I was able to verify that several of the companies listed in the curriculum vitae had been operational at the times she claimed to have been employed, but little else.

The lists of referees were more rewarding and provided me with a starting point in my quest to find out as much as I could about Rebecca's working life both before and after her gender affirmation. Although some of the people listed were no longer alive, and others had long since moved from the addresses given on the curriculum vitae, I was able to contact a surprising number who not only remembered her, but were prepared to talk about the circumstances under which their paths had crossed. Some contacted other former colleagues, passing on the message that Bob Norton's sister was writing her biography, and I was contacted by more old miners, engineers and geologists from across the country, who all had an anecdote to tell.

Through these stories I was able to gain an insight into Rebecca's knowledge and understanding of the mining industry, and the respect in which she was held by the people with whom she worked. None, of course, had any sense that she was grappling with issues around gender and identity, or that her sometimes bizarre behaviour was anything other than attention-seeking.

Nothing these storytellers told me could provide me with a sense of what had motivated her to seek out medical intervention to change gender. She had not told any of them, nor did I raise the topic with her during our late afternoon drinks when we had both returned to Ballarat, although I gleaned snippets of the process she had undergone through her grumblings about the all-male medical practitioners with whom she had dealt over the years, and I knew she was dissatisfied with the service they had provided.

At that time I made a conscious decision not to ask questions. I decided that she needed me more as a sounding board than as an inquisitor, so when it came to writing about this period of Rebecca's life, there was no-one to whom I could talk. Our sister Jan, who was closest to Rebecca during this period of her life, had died in Western Australia of an Asthma attack in 1997. Both our parents had also passed on, not that they could have been prevailed upon to discuss their own reactions to the discovery that the son of whom they had been so proud had always wanted to be their daughter.

I decided to try a different approach – I would search for information about the availability of transgender surgery in Melbourne. This led me first to the 'Gender Dysphoria Clinic' which had been established at the Queen Victoria Hospital in about 1976 and relocated to Monash Medical Centre in 1987 to become the Monash Health Gender Clinic. I made several calls to them, most of which went unanswered, but a scan of newspapers of the time led me to discover that there had been a clinic dealing with gender dysphoria prior to the opening of the Queen Victoria clinic. It was under the direction of Melbourne University Professor Richard Ball, the Chief Psychiatrist at the Parkville Psychiatric Clinic, now part of Victoria's Department of Health. In the hope that Rebecca had been treated there, I applied for her medical records and, to my surprise, I received some 100 pages of notes, letters, medical reports and transcripts of interviews relating to the ten years during which Rebecca had been an outpatient there.

Over nearly two years, Rebecca met regularly with Professor Ball, who recorded answers to the questions he asked about her life at the time. While it made difficult reading, I at last had the sense that I was listening to her tell the story of her life to that point. Through Professor Ball's notes and various other sources, I was also able to uncover the identity of The Captain, so that I could find out more about him and what he meant to Rebecca.

Rebecca's life wasn't all tragedy. There were some highlights, like tunnelling for dinosaurs on the limestone coast. There were mining achievements as well, and according to some of the men with a seat around the table of the various boards of which she was a member, she was highly respected. While the stories they told me went a long way towards filling the gaps in this biography, there remained some holes I simply couldn't fill – only she knows what they contained.

Over all our years together and apart, we had continued to use the diminutives our parents, mostly our father Barney, had used for us. Although I always introduced her as Rebecca to everyone we met once we were both living in Ballarat, she was Rob to me and I was Jilly. I also avoided using the non-binary pronouns of *they* and *their* when talking about her as the concept that for some people gender was undefinable had not been an issue when she committed herself to her transformation. As far as she was concerned she was a woman and that was that.

Consequently, in the first half of this biography, which deals with the life of Robert Michael Norton until February 1974 when her application to change her name by deed poll to Rebecca Michelle Norton was accepted, I will be writing about Rob and using the pronoun *he*, except on the few occasions when I include a passage from Rebecca's later years. The second half of the biography belongs to Rebecca and *she*.

Rob

Margie and Barney

At her first interview with Professor Ball at the Parkville Psychiatric Clinic in October 1974, Rebecca described her father Barney as having had little influence on her life. Her mother Margie, however, had been a dominating presence, prone to lecturing her children on the principles she expected them to uphold, in line with the Roman Catholic beliefs into which they had been baptised. These words, written in the Professor's barely legible scrawl, awakened my own memories of the lectures Rob, Jan and I were subjected to whenever we deviated from the standards Margie expected us to maintain, or when any of us questioned her authority.

I can remember the three of us standing silently in the kitchen of our Skipton Street, Ballarat, home while she berated whichever one of us had fallen short of her expectations, invariably launching into examples of how she had acted in similar circumstances or would have done had she been placed in a similar situation. Our younger siblings, Elizabeth, six years younger than me and Louise, five years younger again, were excluded from these lectures, although they may have been subjected to similar ones after the three of us had left home.

Rob, as Margie's first born and male, who from infancy showed an ability to consume knowledge beyond his years, was the focus of much of the lecturing because she expected him to achieve great things, although in what she could never quite decide. Her expectations for Jan and me were a little more muted, but we were strongly encouraged to seize every opportunity, as she had done when she was invited by the Sisters of Mercy to complete her secondary education at Sacred Heart College, something that was not offered to her nine siblings, who had to make do with the Merit Certificate awarded to students who had satisfactorily completed eight years of schooling at the parish primary schools before they joined the workforce at fourteen years of age.

Margie had matriculated, something few young women of her age achieved, making her eligible to sit the Public Service Examination, which she also passed. That in turn led to employment with the Postmaster General's Department as a telephonist, a highly prized job for a woman in the 1930s. Posted to the Camperdown Telephone Exchange, which serviced the rich Western District pastoral community, she used her fleeting connections with the squattocracy of the district to develop her own sense of superiority.

While marriage into any of the squatter families was never on the cards, principally because most were not Catholics, she certainly had aspirations. She dressed well for the time and considered herself attractive, so that when she met Barney at a dance on one of her visits home to Ballarat, she decided that he was the man for her. He was the most handsome man there, and she had made enquiries of the friends she knew there who told her that his father, for whom he worked, was a prosperous grain merchant and they lived in a two-storey house attached to the Grain Store in Sebastopol.

As she told us the story of how they met and courted over the years until she could transfer to the Post Office in Ballarat, there was a sense, although I doubt any of us were fully aware of it at the time, that Margie felt she had been let down. Although she loved Barney dearly, life had not panned out as she had expected. Barney's father, Charlie Norton, was showing no signs of retiring. Indeed, after having been widowed for several years, he had recently remarried and brought his new wife to live in the Grain Store residence. He never paid his children wages for the work they did for him. They had a roof over their heads and could ask for money when and if they needed it. This meant that, once they were married, Barney had to go cap-in-hand to his father for everything they needed, including the rent for the two-bedroom house in Redan where he and Margie lived for twenty-five years, accommodating all four daughters in one bedroom, and converting the dining room for Rob. Margie, however, made little effort to become part of the Redan community.

The third daughter of an engine driver called Jack O'Farrell she had been born in Box Hill when that now built up suburb of Melbourne was the last stop on the Victorian Railway system, although all of her childhood memories were of Ballarat East where her family moved once Jack was appointed permanently to the Ballarat East Railway yards. They were in good company there. Most of the inhabitants there were Irish or of Irish descent, some of the families being able to claim ancestors who had fought in the Eureka Rebellion of 1854 when the goldminers took on the might of the British Army. Around them and the canvas and daub Catholic Church, the first on the Ballarat goldfields, had developed a town with schools, pubs and a fine brick town hall. There they were largely self-sufficient, and had little need to climb the escarpment to the City of Ballarat where the government institutions built in the wake of the rebellion were surrounded by fine houses occupied by more substantial immigrants to the goldfields, most of whom were not Irish.

Barney's ancestors had come from England, Germany and Scotland, his great grandfather establishing a Hansom Cab service from Sebastopol to the city in the 1860s which he and his son ran until the coming of the trams later in the century put him out of business. He then became a provider for other horse owners establishing a grain store at the end of the tram line in Albert Street. Other immigrants like the Welsh, Cornish and Scots miners made their homes south of the city in Sebastopol and Redan, bringing with them their own traditions and religious beliefs. Some built churches, others chapels, but although Barney was a baptised Catholic, there was no Catholic school or church in the district. What religious instruction he received, he got prior to making his First Communion from the Sisters of Nazareth, who ran a small orphanage on the outskirts of the district.

Rob was born on the 30th December 1940, nine months after Margie and Barney were married, a point Margie always qualified by insisting that he had been three weeks premature lest anyone, including us, should think that she and Barney had not made it to the honeymoon before he was conceived. In her sermons to us she never explained the significance of the nine months, which we would eventually find out via school playground gossip.

Because businesses like Charlie Norton's were considered an essential service, Barney was exempt from enlistment when war was declared in 1939, but that situation changed following the bombing of Darwin in February 1942, with the government belatedly realising that the vast open spaces of Northern Australia were an open invitation to the Japanese, who were expanding rapidly in the region. They announced the formation of a new entity called the Civil Construction Corps, which would be commissioned to build airstrips and other facilities so the defence of the country could be stepped up. The Corps was given the authority to recruit men who could drive trucks and heavy machinery to clear the ground and lay out the runways. Not long after I was born in August 1942, Barney was called up to join the Corps. He would spend the next two years in the Northern Territory with a three week leave break in January 1944, during which time Jan was conceived.

While Barney was a member of the Civil Construction Corps he was receiving a regular wage, most of which was sent to Margie. However, she continued to rail against Charlie Norton throughout our childhood, claiming that he had used Barney's enlistment as an excuse for selling the business, thus depriving Barney of a job when he was granted compassionate leave to return home for Jan's birth, and a few weeks later was demobbed. Instead, he used his knowledge of draught horses to get a job leading

Louise, Elizabeth, Jill, Jan, and Rob (Rebecca)

a horse and dray for the Ballarat Brewing Company. Years later I discovered that my grandfather had not deceived my father. He continued to run the Grain Store in Sebastopol until well after the war ended, selling it as a going concern in 1947.

Another bone of contention for Margie was the fact that those who served in the Civil Construction Corps were ineligible for the cheap home loans, scholarships and other benefits awarded to men who had served the country in the armed services. Barney progressed from leading a team of brewery horses to driving a truck for a cartage company operating out of the old bluestone goods sheds at Ballarat Railway Station and then to delivering parcels for the Myer Department Store in Ballarat, but money was always tight. We were, nevertheless, well-schooled in not letting our poverty show. Our clothes, particularly school uniforms and what we wore to church on Sundays were treated with great care so they would last until we grew out of them, which I was always slow to do. By the time I was eight and Jan was six, she was taller than me and would go on to be as tall as Rob and Barney, which meant I rarely got anything new, until I learnt how to make my own clothes.

A Good Catholic Education

Formal education for Rob and me began at the little school in the grounds of our parish church, St. Aloysius in Redan. Rob had just turned five when he started in 1946 and I joined him the following year when I was not quite four and a half, the two of us walking the kilometre or so from our home in Skipton Street along the side of the road, as there were no made footpaths at that time. There was also nowhere to shelter along the way, so if it was raining we arrived at the school dripping wet.

The school was run by the Sisters of Loreto, two of whom were driven out each morning from their principal residence at Loreto Abbey, Mary's Mount, the magnificent building on the shores of Lake Wendouree which had been gifted to the group of nuns sent out from their convent in Dublin in 1875 by the first bishop of Ballarat, Michael O'Connor. In the first of the classrooms at St Aloysius, one of the sisters taught Infants and Grades One and Two, while the other sister was responsible for teaching girls up to and including the Merit Certificate in the second classroom. At the time it was considered improper for religious sisters to teach boys beyond the age of eight. They needed the firm hand of the Christian Brothers.

My memory of the classroom Rob and I occupied is faded, but I do recall that there were three rows of desks, one for each of the grades. Each desk accommodated two children, but I don't recall anything about the child who sat beside me. I do know that Rob sat in the front desk of the middle Grade One row. All teaching was done by rote, with senior girls from the other classroom acting as monitors to assist the teacher.

With his six-year-old photographic memory already switched on, Rob was quickly able to absorb everything being taught to his class as well as giving him ample time to listen in to the Grade Two lessons. By the end of the year he knew everything being taught across the whole classroom, prompting the teacher to recommend to Margie that he should move immediately to Grade Three at the Brothers.

Margie was quite familiar with the Christian Brothers who, having been founded to teach poor boys in Cork at the turn of the 19th century, had found ready acceptance among Catholics of Irish descent in places like Ballarat, where they had opened primary schools and taken over the running of the only Catholic secondary school for boys in the region.

There was no suggestion on the first day Margie walked Rob to St Patrick's Primary School, known to everyone at the time as 'Drummo' because it was on the corner of Drummond and Eyre Streets, that there was any reason to be apprehensive for her son's welfare. She knew he would be able to handle the curriculum without difficulty, and his behaviour was such that he was unlikely to incur the wrath of the brothers for any other reason, even though they were renowned for the physical punishment they meted out to any boy who did not meet their exacting standards.

As Rob was leaving St Aloysius, Margie decided it was time I left too. For the next few years I caught the tram into the city to attend the day school for girls run by the Loreto nuns in Dawson Street. Jan joined me the following year, but our stay there was fairly short. In the middle of 1951, Margie became so dissatisfied with the progress we were making that she whisked us both over to Sacred Heart College, two tram rides away in Ballarat East, so that we could experience the kind of quality education she had received from the Sisters of Mercy.

Once Rob and I were at separate schools, communication between us diminished considerably. It was as if we were living in two separate spheres: Jan and I in one and Rob and his school friends in another. A bike had been procured for him, not a new one, but he could ride to school and to the houses of the boys he knew. He was never encouraged to bring any of them home, as Margie did not welcome the neighbours into her house, probably for fear that they would find out how poor we were.

Although I knew Rob was achieving well at school and had been invited into a select little group of special boys which the brother in charge of Drummo had gathered around him, I had no idea what its purpose was, only that they went to the school on Saturdays to help with chores that could not be done during the week, and were taken on occasional picnics as a reward. It wasn't until I started to piece together our childhoods so I could write about Rob's early years, that I discovered the school principal's name was McCarthy.

McCarthy! The name Rebecca had snarled at her television screen on the 19th May 2015, the day the Royal Commission into Institutional Responses to Child Sexual Abuse began hearing submissions in Ballarat. I had been sitting in the room she had occupied at Kirralee Nursing Home for the previous two years listening to her obsess about the possibility that the nursing staff would on this particular occasion forget to bring her daily bottle of champagne at 3pm. The television was on with the sound down, but the cameras were focussed on the crowd building in front of the Ballarat Court House. As I didn't know if she had been following the revelations about paedophilia in the Catholic institutions we had been familiar with as we were growing up I said, 'The Royal Commission is in Ballarat today.'

She stopped obsessing, climbed off her bed and padded her way across the room to the television, peering closely at the image on the screen as if looking for a familiar face. 'Are they calling McCarthy?' she snarled.

I remember saying, 'Who's McCarthy?' but she didn't answer. She had gone back to obsessing about her champagne.

From the archives of St Patrick's Cathedral and St. Patrick's College, I was able to obtain school photos of an angelic looking Rob in neat uniform usually sitting in the front row of the class. These also gave me the names of the Christian Brothers who were teaching there during Rob's time at the school. There were only four of them, each taking a composite class of two-year groups with upwards of 100 boys in each classroom. All learning was by rote as it was the only way, along with the strap the brothers wore attached to the belt of their religious habit, that they could maintain order.

While some boys left the school after Grade 6 to continue their education at St Patrick's College, the majority continued to Grade 8 and sat for their Merit Certificate, by which time they were nearing their 14th birthday and could legally leave school, get a job or begin an apprenticeship. McCarthy taught Grades 7 & 8 and also had overall authority over the running of the school. That meant he could issue punishments for playground infringements, failure to have the correct school uniform, and for any other offence which came to his attention. He could also single out boys who met his criteria for good students.

Initially it was hard to find out anything about James Philip McCarthy. From the Archivist at St Patrick's College I discovered that he had been appointed Principal of Drummo in 1949, walking there every morning from the College where all the brothers lived. She referred me to the Archivist for the Christian Brothers Order who sent me two articles from their necrology. Both were compilations of memories written by members of the Order who had lived or worked alongside him or had been taught by him. The picture they all painted of this austere, prematurely white-haired brother was one of dedication to the teaching profession and to the Catholic ethos. Some of the contributors did admit, though, that he was a strict taskmaster who demanded exact obedience to his rule.

From the Archivist for the Cathedral I learnt more. He had attended Drummo a few years after Rob and had been one of the special boys. He showed me photos taken by McCarthy who was a keen photographer, with his own dark room in the building in which he lived at the College. The photos were taken during a session one Saturday when the boys were supposed to be tidying the dress-up cupboard. This activity apparently involved the boys stripping off to their underpants and draping themselves with items from the cupboard while McCarthy took black and white snaps. The photos I saw were of a little blonde-haired boy of about eight years of age, naked to the waist, with a thin strip of sheer material draped over his head and one shoulder. Apparently, this boy's mother had proudly kept the snaps, oblivious to any implications which would have been associated with them today. If Rob was ever given photos, he did not bring them home, but the activity must have had a dramatic effect on him, as he told Professor Ball that he had begun having feelings that he was in the wrong gender at about this time.

From another man who had been at Drummo at about the same time, I learnt about McCarthy's more violent streak. He punished boys for any minor transgression, either by humiliating them or by means of a cane which he used in preference to the leather strap. One boy, made to spend the day in his underpants for forgetting his sports shorts, thought himself fortunate not to get the cane across his buttocks.

It was not until the report of the Royal Commission into Institutional Responses to Child Sexual Abuse was published in December 2017, a few months after Rebecca died, that I learnt the extent of McCarthy's offences against children in his care. He hounded boys who broke the school rules or otherwise offended him, subjecting them to frequent beatings on their bare backsides or thighs. For the most recalcitrant of his victims, however, he was prepared to trade corporal punishment for sexual gratification. In the privacy of the music room which he took as his private fiefdom, boys would be made to masturbate him.

If Rob knew what McCarthy was capable of, or was even fearful that he could suffer the same abuse, it would seem that he never discussed his fears at home. He probably accepted that any criticism of the brothers would not be tolerated by Margie who, like so many good Catholics at the time, thought that the priests and religious brothers and sisters, having taken a vow of celibacy, were incapable of such evil.

For his loyalty, good behaviour and ability, Rob was offered a fee-free place at St Patrick's College once he had completed Grade Eight at Drummo, but it came with provisions. Year Nine, or Sub Intermediate as it was called then, had two streams – one for boys who had been enrolled at the College since Grade Six and the other for boys from the district whether or not they had been taught by the Christian Brothers in the parish primary schools. The assumption was made that these boys were destined to remain at the College only until they had completed their Intermediate certificate, which was considered an adequate qualification for them to progress to employment in a bank or office. For this reason, they were not offered Advanced Maths or Latin.

The only Latin Rob knew consisted of the responses he made as an altar boy at Mass at St Aloysius, which had been learnt by heart under the mentorship of the head altar boy Gerald Ridsdale, who was several years older than the boys he was training and destined for the priesthood himself. He would go on to become the most notorious paedophile in Australia, but if he was already molesting the boys in his care during the time Rob served on the altar, there was no mention of it at home. To Margie he was a fine example of a boy from a good Catholic family.

Nor did the parish priest seem to have any concerns about the relationship between his head altar boy and the boys he was training. The priest, who was from the west coast of Ireland and had trained at All Hallows College in Dublin, where being able to speak English was not a prerequisite, and the theology course was described as short and practical, was a regular visitor to our home, where he would stay for hours, drinking cups of tea and warming his backside against the wood stove. He probably considered these visits to our home and others in the parish as his pastoral duty, but there was little or no pastoral advice handed out as he sampled the parish cooking skills.

Occasionally, all the altar boys from the churches in Ballarat were required to participate in grand liturgical celebrations at St Patrick's Cathedral. It was at these that Rob first encountered the head altar boy of the Cathedral, George Pell. Although a year younger than Rob, he stood head and shoulders over him and the rest of the boys from the parishes. And judging by the reaction any mention of him evoked in Rob later in life, he was a bully even then.

Once Rob was at St Pat's though, their paths rarely crossed. While Pell was destined for great things on the sporting field, with Victorian Football League talent scouts vying for the opportunity to sign him up, Rob was hopeless at football and managed to wriggle his way out of training by running errands for the legendary football coach Brother Bill O'Malley.

Rob was still under fourteen in September 1954 and was therefore eligible to take the Junior Government Scholarship Examinations, which were held at the Ballarat Town Hall over two days – English and Mathematics on the first day and General Knowledge on the following morning. His name was among the successful candidates published in the *Ballarat Courier* in December of the same year. As well as meeting the tuition fees, the scholarship came with a clothing and book allowance, which eased the pressure on the finances at home.

Rob's academic results for his first year at the College could not be ignored by the College hierarchy, who promoted him to the A stream for his Intermediate year, despite the fact that he had no Latin and only General Mathematics. That posed no problem for Rob, who immersed himself in the Latin textbook until he knew the ancient language as well as the boys who had been learning it for three years. By the end of the year he had easily surpassed them. It was the same with mathematics. In the Intermediate Certificate exams which were conducted externally by the Victorian Education Department, he passed Maths A and B and Arithmetic as well as Latin, English Expression and Literature, History, Geography and Science. He was second overall in the class and was awarded the Scholastic Prize at the College prize-giving night.

As the brothers expected, there was a mass exodus from the College after the Intermediate year, so there were only enough students remaining for one class of boys doing their Leaving Certificates. Once again, Rob was obliged to do Latin, but he also took on two Advanced Mathematics subjects as well as Physics and Chemistry, excelling at all of them.

Well before Rob's brilliance had begun to shine, though, he was already receiving preferential treatment within our home, which was a small rented cottage with only two bedrooms. As it was deemed improper for him to share sleeping arrangements with Jan and I, the dining room, which was never used as such as we did not have a dining room table and no-one was ever invited to share a meal with us, became his bedroom. It evolved into his exclusive domain once Margie decided that he could not be expected to do his homework at the kitchen table with Jan and me. Barney, who by this time was driving the delivery van for Myer, had brought home a desk which had been discarded by one of the managers, and a chair and bookshelf had also been found, probably from the same source. The only time I could go into the room was if there was sewing needing to be done. Then I had access to the Singer treadle sewing machine which sat just inside the door.

The rules changed slightly once a set of encyclopedias which, although somewhat out of date, arrived and were treated with great respect by the whole family. First published in 1933 under the title *Richards Cyclopedia* in New

York, and edited by Mary and Ernest Wright, the set consisted of fifteen volumes, the last of which was an index. The remaining volumes were not arranged alphabetically but by subject under the headings of science, social studies, industry, art, biography, and leisure activities. Each volume comprised many short articles on particular subtopics and were all well illustrated. Volume 14 was our favourite. Titled Leisure-time Activities, it contained articles about manual arts, games and sports, fairy tales, fables, stories, myths.

While Jan and I were allowed to take Volume 14 off the shelf and carry it reverently to the kitchen so we could pore over Aesop's Fables and Grimms Fairy Stories, Rob had the rest of the volumes to himself. These he read from cover to cover, storing away bits of information with which to impress Margie and Barney at the dinner table on a nightly basis.

There were no other books of note in the house except for the ones we withdrew from the Ballarat Municipal Library once a fortnight. As children we were allowed one book each which was more than enough for me with my poor eyesight and undiagnosed dyslexia. By the time I had reached the end page, Rob had not only read the book he had borrowed but everybody else's as well, even Margie's which were written by novelists like Daphne du Maurier and Catherine Gaskin.

Barney's selections were probably more to Rob's liking as they were adventure stories, often set in Northern Australia or the islands to the north of the country. One of his favourite authors was Ion L Idriess whose books were often about the daring do of well-known figures such as

Flynn of the Outback and Lassiter's Last Ride. Frank Dalby Davison was another whose books I remember Barney and Rob reading.

By the time Rob was beginning his Leaving Certificate year I had begun Sub Intermediate. I pleaded for a desk under the window in the bedroom I shared by this stage with Jan, Liz and Louise, but it was some years before one was found for me. That didn't stop me from trying to outshine Rob with my subject choices. Although I couldn't learn Latin because it wasn't taught at Sacred Heart College, I did French and German and I added Biology to the list of science subjects, but it wasn't enough to convince Margie that I was at least as competent as he was.

Jan didn't compete with either of us. She had made up her mind as soon as she entered secondary school that she would be staying only as long as it would take her to gain the necessary secretarial skills to get a job. No amount of lecturing on Margie's part would change her mind, so she was reluctantly allowed to leave school once she had completed her Intermediate Certificate, as long as Barney could get her a job in the Myer typing pool where he could keep an eye on her. Within a couple of years she had transferred to Myer Melbourne and soon afterwards had become a secretary to one of the directors.

Career Options

Despite his excellent results in the Leaving examinations, staying on at St Pat's to matriculate was not an option for a working-class boy like Rob. The Brothers expected most of the boys who completed matriculation to be accepted into Law, Medicine or the Arts like their fathers, who were usually old boys of the College and had gone on to study at Melbourne University. There was also a handful of boys each year who chose to enter the priesthood or religious orders.

The options for boys like Rob were not so glamorous. They could seek employment in the office of one of the many Ballarat solicitors as an Articled Clerk, and embark on years of night school and distance education to eventually complete a law degree, with the expectation that they would gain employment with the law firm at which they had been articled. Alternatively, they could choose to become a primary school teacher, completing the two- or three-year courses at the Ballarat Teachers' College. A third option was a diploma in Engineering or Applied Sciences at the Ballarat School of Mines.

Even if Rob had shown interest in taking the Articled Clerk road to becoming a lawyer, places were hard to find and usually went to boys whose parents had business dealings with the local law firms, which Margie and Barney certainly did not. While there were bursaries available to study teaching, those who took them were tied to the Department of Education for several years once they graduated and had little choice in the location of the schools to which they were posted. Besides, Margie believed that primary school teaching was a waste of Rob's ability.

That left only the Ballarat School of Mines (SMB), which sat perched on the top of the hill in Lydiard Street South. Established in 1870 at a time when the alluvial gold that had attracted miners from the four corners of the world to Ballarat was nearing exhaustion, the School of Mines initially provided training in the skills needed by the new breed of miners who were amalgamating to exploit the quartz leads which ran beneath the basalt plateau. Over the years more courses were added, not just to cater for the miners but for industry generally, becoming one of a handful of highly regarded Senior Technical Colleges in Victoria. By the time Rob had enrolled at the School of Mines, the school had grown, spreading down the Dana Street Hill in a series of mismatched buildings linked by staircases and crooked paths to Albert Street below. It also stretched out along the top of the ridge surrounding the old Gaol, which still housed a motley collection of prisoners, mainly vagrants who found it convenient to be arrested before the winter set in.

Opposite the school's main building sat the Ballarat Brewery, home to Ballarat Bertie, whose image appeared on all the bottles the brewery produced, and on hoardings around the city, even after it had been taken over by

Carlton and United Breweries in 1958. It was still operating as a brewery long after Rob and I passed through the School of Mines, but its buildings and grounds would also eventually be absorbed into the technical school which would itself be absorbed into the Ballarat College of Advanced Education which was the forerunner of Ballarat University and then Federation University.

As most of the students who enrolled at the School of Mines in 1957 had come from one of several junior technical schools in the region, where they had completed the equivalent of the Intermediate Certificate, the first year of all the courses on offer contained the same core subjects of Physics, Chemistry, and Advanced Mathematics, together with a couple of subjects relating to individual specialties. This meant that Rob was repeating what he already knew, giving him ample time to devote to the subjects specific to his chosen discipline of Civil Engineering such as Metallurgy and Geology. Not content with mastering these, he also embarked on studying the Mining Engineering electives, passing them all with flying colours. It is probable that Margie and Barney were unaware that he was intending to achieve diplomas in both disciplines until the end of the first year, when he was awarded the prize for having the highest marks across all disciplines and was also awarded the inaugural Josephine Brelaz Prize for Science. This prize, in the form of a scholarship to be awarded annually to the student who showed the greatest merit, had been founded in memory of their mother by brothers Guido and Noel Brelaz, both of whom had been diploma students at the School of Mines. Rob would win the Prize again in 1960.

He was also eligible to apply for a Commonwealth Scholarship which, of course, he was awarded. As it came with a means-tested living allowance of £130 per annum it was most welcome, and it meant that he needed little assistance from Margie and Barney over the next few years. While it didn't appear obvious at the time, there was a marked relaxation in the austerity levels at home. As my fees at Sacred Heart College were also paid for by the scholarship I had won at the end of Grade Eight, only those of Jan and Liz had to be found out of Barney's pay packet until Louise started school.

While Margie couldn't have been happier with Rob's initial achievements at the School of Mines, she worried that his spiritual wellbeing was no longer being guided, as it had been under the Brothers. To ensure that he was not too influenced by the godless atmosphere of the School of Mines she insisted that he join the St. Patrick's Cathedral chapter of the Young Christian Workers (YCW) and attend the activities they conducted for the youth of the diocese.

This organisation had started in Belgium in the 1920s with the aim of providing guidance for Catholic youth entering the workforce. It had been transported to Australia after World War II and was tasked with nurturing the Catholic ethos in the young of the dioceses in which it operated through regular spiritual guidance tempered with social and sporting activities. Until he left Ballarat at the end of 1960, Rob regularly attended meetings and other activities more, as he told Professor Ball in 1973, because it was easier to comply with Margie's insistence that he do so than to oppose her. He also told Ball that he had only been subject to one lecture on sex education in his life and that it had been delivered by one of Ballarat's Catholic doctors on behalf of the YCW.

The YCW also provided Rob with the opportunity to chase his dream of becoming a champion cross-country runner. During the 1956 Olympics he stood watching grainy black and white television in the windows of the Myer store on Sturt Street. Although disappointed that his hero the great Emil Zatopek was unable to compete at his best due to injury, he was thrilled by the performances of the mostly Eastern European runners who scooped up medals in the distance events. He joined the YCW Harriers in the winter of his first year at SMB.

The Harriers were an odd assortment of runners ranging from swift young lads around Rob's age to some quite old men who shuffled along at the rear of the pack. There was quite a following of mothers, wives and girlfriends who cheered them on and served cups of tea, cake and sandwiches when the race was over. Margie never came to watch Rob run, sending me in her stead. I hated it – I was too young and too dowdily dressed for the girlfriends to notice me, and the women did not want me listening in to their conversations. I dried dishes, picked up rubbish and hurried home as soon as I could after each race was over.

After the first couple of winters, my services were no longer required, presumably at Rob's insistence, though I was not privy to this rare act of defiance on his part. He must have experienced considerable anxiety when Margie decided that I would be studying the Diploma of Applied Chemistry at the School of Mines, but not until I had matriculated from Sacred Heart College. This meant we wouldn't have to be under the same academic roof until the beginning of 1960, his final year.

Applied Chemistry had not been my choice – I had wanted to be a nurse, but Margie would have none of it. She had plenty of reasons why nursing was not a suitable career for me. I was too small for a start and I had had a brush with rheumatic fever when I was 14. Once the decision was made for me, I took all the subjects needed for the Diploma – Pure and Applied Mathematics, Chemistry and Physics. I also added Biology and I began to look forward to studying at the School of Mines.

Well before I started there in February 1960 though, Rob made it abundantly clear to me that I was not to speak to him or even acknowledge my relationship to him on campus. I could not expect any help if I was in difficulties and I certainly could not take part in any activities in which he was involved. If Margie was aware of the strictures placed on me she certainly did not intervene. I think neither she nor Barney had any idea of the extent of Rob's involvement in student activities. I only discovered that once classes for the year had started and I was able to observe from a distance the clusters of students surrounding him outside the main building during lunchtime. He was the life and soul of the place, always talking, always attracting an audience.

The male students had access to an activities room called the Stud Room, which was an old hall situated between the main administrative building and the Wesley Church, but it was off limits for the three female students studying Chemistry. After many complaints from us we were begrudgingly given a room of our own, little more than a broom cupboard, attached to the outside wall of the Stud Room. Through the brick wall separating us, I would often hear Rob's voice followed by peals of laughter from the students he was addressing.

I soon discovered that he was by this time President of the Student Representative Council, Editor of the student magazine, Captain of the athletics team and was well on the way to becoming the School of Mines' champion raconteur. I would only discover how this transformation had taken place when I began to refresh my memory of our time at the School of Mines by reading the back copies of *SMB, the* student magazine, which I found in the Geoffrey Blainey Research Centre of Federation University. The general consensus from the magazine contributors was that Rob had had something of a baptism during his six-week work experience at Mount Morgan in Central Queensland.

It was the policy of the School of Mines that all technical students should do work experience in their chosen field during the summer vacation. Rob chose Mount Morgan, inland from Rockhampton in Central Queensland, as did another student whose article about the experience I read in SMB magazine. According to the unnamed writer, the mine and the town where the workforce lived were in their death throes by the time they arrived, after two days of travel which involved train journeys from Ballarat to Melbourne and then to Sydney, where they caught a train to Brisbane and another to Rockhampton. They and a handful of other students from various technical colleges across the country were picked up at Rockhampton Station by a maniacal bus driver for the final leg of their journey to Mount Morgan. For Rob, who had never been further than Melbourne on a train, this must have been exhausting. And then to be hit by the stench of rotting mangoes mixed with the sulfurous gasses coming from the slag heaps was more than the article writer could cope with. But Rob was not deterred.

Originally a rich underground gold mine, by the end of 1958 Mount Morgan was operating as an open cut mine, mainly for copper. The students were put to work on a variety of tasks, none of which enhanced their knowledge of mining to any great extent, and at night they were treated to the spectacular sight of the waste sulfurous acid being burnt off. As it was the wet season, they experienced frequent downpours, which brought the walls of ore crashing down with thunderous roars. The town itself was so dead that, apart from an occasional film at the picture theatre, there was no night life, and the students had to make do with their own company.

The writer of the article did not elaborate on how the experience of six weeks in alien surroundings, with only the company of other students who had all been strangers to each other at the beginning of their stay had changed Rob, but it certainly had.

There were plenty of references to Rob's transformation in the pages of the 1960 edition of SMB magazine. In a report into the presentation of the Pomeroy Cup, awarded in honour of Frank Pomeroy, who had been a past Chemistry student and a champion footballer, 'Claude' wrote that although no-one would be able to surpass Pomeroy in the art of 'bulldusting', Robert Norton was an unlikely but deserving winner. He wrote:

> The interest centres on the fact that last year not a word was heard from him. This year, however, he burst into the scene with some of the most eloquent bulldusting ever heard, in subjects such as sport, women, etc. (chiefly women). His fine form is said to be due to vocational experience at Mount Morgan. Although he lacked the wide range of subjects of Mr Pomeroy, his knowledge of certain subjects was outstanding in that it was complete and utter bull.

The trophy, an old jam tin welded onto a stand, did not make it home to grace the dining room mantelpiece.

There were also several references to Rob's discovery of women throughout the magazine and of him being a serial nuisance at the Teachers' College Hostel, which was supervised by a Mrs Moore, who was habitually having to chase him off the premises after curfew. This behaviour featured in a poem which contained verses dedicated to each of the diploma students who would be finishing at the end of 1960. Rob managed two verses.

> Norton WAS quiet,
> Would never be named
> But for women and 'CUP'
> a W.O.W he's acclaimed.

The second verse, I was told, related to the impression Rob gave of being a 'Pearl Pureheart'. He didn't drink, smoke or swear. Nor would he listen to a dirty joke and, according to one of the graduating students who knew him well, was almost certainly a virgin.

> Bob is a man,
> He likes good clean fun,
> But he'll see what he missed
> When he's too old to run.

By the time the magazine with its little verses and other comments made it home, if it ever did, Rob had moved on to university, so Margie could not ask him what the verses meant. She was well aware of his interest in girls which she probably accepted as normal, although she probably would have preferred that he was meeting good Catholic girls rather than those who were studying to be state primary school teachers. She did persuade him to partner a few girls at the debutante balls which were a feature of diocesan life in Ballarat, with each parish hosting an annual event. He partnered our cousin Helen when she made her debut and took her to at least one other ball, and he probably benefited from the training he got from the usually officious women who conducted the training sessions leading up to each ball. But he almost certainly found the Teachers' College girls much more fun than the debutantes.

A few months after Rebecca died, I was given the contact details of an old engineer who had been at SMB with him, and I asked what the verses in the magazine referred to. He didn't know – it was too long ago, he said – but he was aware that Rob had undergone a gender change. There had been a reunion of sorts a few years previously of as many of that cohort of students who were still contactable, but no-one knew how to get in touch with Rob. The old engineer did circulate my request for information for the biography I planned to write, and several more past students got in touch. While their memories were faded, they did all talk about the Rob they knew in fond terms.

Most wanted to remind me of Rob's contribution to the stage productions at SMB. Started in 1958 by the chain-smoking English lecturer Eric McGrath, Rob had only a small part in that first revue, but after his spell in Mount Morgan he seemed ready to spread his wings on stage. Not only was he one of the main performers in the second revue, he also involved himself in the skills needed to stage a production. By 1960 he was Stage Manager, for which he was soundly praised by one of the writers for the SMB magazine.

He didn't impress everyone though. Not long after the 1960 Revue had been staged, Jan and I were walking home from Mass at St Patrick's on a cold Sunday morning when we were joined by Teddy. I didn't know his other name and still don't, but I had seen him around the school, so he was obviously a student. Jan knew him from the Saturday night dances which she went to regularly now that she was a working girl, having been employed in the typing pool at Myer for about six months.

Teddy was extraordinarily good looking with a wonderful head of black curly hair as I recall. We started talking about the revue and Rob's role in its success. We had reached the corner of Sebastopol and Skipton Streets by this time, so he left us with, 'Your brother's a queen'.

He was gone up Sebastopol Street before either of us

could ask him what he meant, so we kept walking along Skipton Street in silence. We had no words to deal with what he had said and there was nobody we could ask!

I did ask the old engineers if they had been aware of anything in Rob's behaviour that may have indicated that he was grappling with his gender identity. They hadn't, but all added that in 1960, when they were just reaching their twenties, they were innocents who knew very little about such matters.

There was, however, another topic which was much easier to broach with them – 'The Great Gaol Break'. It had taken place around the same time as the Revue and it had sent a ripple of excitement through the whole establishment. While the old engineers were all keen to play down their part in the discovery of the tunnel leading from a disused storeroom in the basement of the old courthouse where the engineers had many of their classes, they did admit to being members of the digging party. The tunnel had been filled with rubble and sealed with a locked door, which the students had forced open, and then started an excavation process similar to the one described by Australian fighter pilot, prisoner of war, and author Paul Brickhill in his 1950 epic account of the Great Escape from Stalag III which became the basis of the film by the same name in 1963.

While the teaching staff were aware that their students were behaving strangely, they were unable to discover the cause until a manhole cover began to rise in the Gaol exercise yard balanced on the head of a student. There was much consternation among the prison guards and their prisoners, who had no desire to use the tunnel to mount an escape. Once the alarm was given, the Board of Works was called in and the tunnel was concreted over, but not before the local newspaper the *Ballarat Courier* had been down to get the story. None of Rob's old friends could remember what part Rob played in the whole affair, but they were sure he was there.

Untying the Apron Strings

Sometime towards the end of 1960, it was decided that Rob should complete a degree in Engineering at Melbourne University. Who made the decision I don't know, but I suspect that the senior lecturers in the Engineering Department of the School of Mines had made the initial recommendation, based on his academic record over the previous four years, that Rob be admitted into the third year of the degree course at the University.

Despite the realisation that Rob would remain at least partially dependent on Margie and Barney for another two years, the news of a place at the University was welcomed at home. He would be the first of the extended family to gain a university degree, with the exception of Margie's cousin Barry Blake, who was well on his way to a distinguished career as a linguist. The impact on the family finances was minimised by the extension of Rob's Commonwealth Scholarship which had sustained him over the previous three years, especially as it would now provide a living away from home allowance. The only issue left to be dealt with was where Rob would reside in Melbourne.

He showed little interest in this issue, leaving Margie to deal with it while he completed his final examinations at the School of Mines before heading north to gain more work experience, this time at Mount Isa. Getting there was even more arduous than the journey to Mount Morgan the previous year, necessitating several train journeys to Townsville and then inland to Cloncurry and Mt Isa itself, taking the best part of five days to complete. But for Rob the jolting of the carriages and the sleepless nights were all worthwhile. He fell instantly in love with Mount Isa.

Unlike the Mount Morgan Mining Company, which seemed to treat work experience students as a source of cheap labour for which they had little responsibility, Mount Isa Mines ran a comprehensive training program designed to introduce the students, who came from universities and technical colleges across the country and beyond, to the various aspects of the mining and refining processes being undertaken by the company, so as to acquaint them with the working conditions they were likely to encounter if they chose a career in mining.

As well as attending a series of lectures given by experienced personnel, the students were taken on tours of the mine's various operations including the copper open cut mine at Black Rock, the ore handling, crushing, and smelting operations and the miles of underground tunnels reached by descending shafts sunk deep into the ground. They visited other mines in the region, including the mothballed Mary Kathleen Uranium Mine in the Selwyn Range between Mt. Isa and Cloncurry. They then had to take the exam that all potential employees of the mine took before they were assigned to a work detail.

The Management of Mount Isa Mines took a paternalistic interest in the students temporarily in their employ by complementing the training program with one that introduced these young men, and they were all men in the 1960s, to the social aspects of the town. It boasted an Olympic-sized swimming pool, bowling greens, a couple of picture theatres, one of them a drive-in, tennis courts and, for the more adventurous, there were the water sports on the recently opened Lake Moondarra, six kilometres from town, which had been formed by the damming of the Leichhardt River. Dances, picnics and barbeques were arranged so the students could meet the townsfolk and learn from them what it was like to live in far North Queensland in a mining setting.

Rob returned from this period of work experience just in time to move into Newman College, the Jesuit run Catholic college at the University, but as I had been in Melbourne for the whole of the summer holidays doing work experience at the Royal Women's Hospital in Carlton, I had no idea who had been responsible for finding the accommodation and how prestigious it was. My only interest was in whether I could have Rob's desk and sole use of the dining room now that he was not living at home. Unfortunately, Margie assumed, quite wrongly as it turned out, that Rob would come home during study breaks and would need his room to be just as he had left it.

It wasn't until I began searching for information about Rob's two years at Melbourne University that I gave any thought to the fact that he was living at one of a handful of privately run and expensive colleges within the University. I presume that Margie had gathered together letters from St Patrick's College, the Monsignor from the

Cathedral and from our very Catholic doctor, who had probably lived at Newman during his student days, to accompany the letter of application she had written to Newman College on Rob's behalf, but I had no idea how she expected to pay the fees the College charged for the accommodation, tutoring and guidance the priests provided to the students in their care.

Although it was nearly sixty years since Rob had lived at Newman, I decided to phone the College on the off-chance that someone had been keeping records all this time. I spoke to the Provost, who was reluctant to provide me with any details unless I could prove my relationship to the person about whom I was enquiring. This was the first, but certainly not the last time I had to provide proof that I had a right to ask for and receive archival information about Rob.

I gathered up birth and death certificates, power of attorney documents and Rebecca's will and had certified copies made, one set of which I sent to the Provost along with a copy of the short biography I had prepared for the relatives and friends who had attended Rebecca's wake, so he would see for himself that the Robert Michael Norton about whom I was enquiring was the same person as the Rebecca Michelle Norton whose name appeared on the certified documents. He rang me almost immediately he received them requesting permission to publish an extract from the biography in the Obituary column of the College's annual magazine.

I gave permission and was surprised when he sent me a copy of the Newman College Newsletter for 2017 to find that he had published the biography in full and had included the photo I had used of Rebecca with her two dogs Amber and Tabatha. In a subsequent phone call, he suggested that Rob's stay at the college may have been funded by one of the many bursaries and scholarships donated by generous old boys that the Rector had at his disposal.

While the Provost could not give me any information about unauthorised activities the students of Rob's era got up to, he took it upon himself to track down a couple of men who had been students at the College at the same time. They were happy to talk to me, but could tell me little except that they remembered Rob as a very friendly and amiable person with whom it was always very easy to have a good chat. One of them began telling me about a prank which took place one night in Whitehorse Road, Box Hill. He promised to send me the details but never did, despite a couple of follow up phone calls. Perhaps Rob was involved, perhaps not.

Both the Provost and the two former students directed me to the Newman College Newsletters for 1961 and 1962, both of which had been digitised. The Students' Club ran a number of events during 1961 including a ball and a theatrical production of the play *Charley's Aunt*. Rob's name was not among the cast or even the production team. Nor was he in the athletics team which competed in the inter-college sports. His name did not appear in the lists of students who took part in the Sodality of Our Lady or the debating club either.

In 1962 Rob did have a part in the theatrical production for that year of the play *Montserrat* by Lillian Hellman, which revolved around the rebellion led by Simon Bolivar against the Spanish Occupation of South America. According to those responsible for writing the humorous farewells for finishing students featured in the *Valete* page at the rear of the magazine:

> Bob ... endeared himself to us with his bonhomie and acting ability – in that order. Of his bonhomie we can say that there was more 'homie' than 'bon'; of his acting ability we can say that there was more acting than ability.

While the polite young men of Newman College couldn't bring themselves to use the word 'bulldust' or worse 'bullshit', he was in their eyes 'a distinguished *Oxologist* and doyen of tipple-tattlers'. In perhaps the only suggestion that during his time at Newman Rob was also dealing with issues to do with his gender, the *Valete* writers had added the following line: 'When the drama of his own life seemed insufficient he sought for catharsis in the ersatz thrills and spills of the speed-car amphitheatre'.

The former students could throw no light on what was meant by that remark, nor did they seem to know where the speed-car amphitheatre was. After some searching, I discovered that speedcar racing had had a presence in Melbourne since 1935 when the first Championship was run at the Tracey Speedway in Maribyrnong, which was still operating in the 1960s. There were other tracks, including one closer to the city at what was to become Olympic Park, and another at Brooklyn, but what interested me was what was driving Rob to find catharsis by watching cars going around a racetrack and what the drama in his life was that he needed to escape from it in such a fashion. I was left to wonder if the polite young men of Newman College were aware that all was not as it seemed with Rob's sexuality or whether they, like the majority of students studying engineering at the University who had matriculated at prestigious Melbourne colleges and schools, saw people like Rob with his Technical College diplomas as country bumpkins.

According to the Engineering Department annual for 1962 called *Nuts and Cranks*, of which I was eventually able to obtain a copy once they had completed the digitising project on which they had embarked to occupy the staff during the Covid epidemic, the students who joined the degree course in third year were referred to as *blockos*. This derogatory term had originally referred to the returned servicemen from World War II who had been allocated small parcels of largely marginal farming land as recompense for their service. As many had no previous experience in farming, they were committing themselves and their families to a life of hardship and poverty.

While Rob could wear a suit, tie and academic gown to dinner at Newman or to the Education Faculty events, his lack of sophistication was clearly on show in everything else he did. It spilled over into his lack of ease with the girls from the women's colleges as one of the Newman *Valete* writers exposed with the quip in the Taboo section of the 1962 Newsletter: 'S.Y.T. (to Norton): I love your eyes – those lovely red eyes'.

Rather than go into his shell, Rob did the opposite. He sought attention by being involved in whatever prank he could worm his way into and spent large amounts of time watching speedcars go around a track. When he was not there, he was at the Clyde Hotel in Carlton, the regular drinking hole of generations of Engineering students from the University, as the only entry I could find for him in *Nuts and Cranks* would attest:

> 43.-NORTON, R. M.
> Born Ballarat 1941 in usual way. Educated at St. Patricks College and then School of Mines Ballarat. Was a keen and conscientious student and became proud possessor of Civil and Mining Diplomas. Was a good athlete but now trains regularly at the Clyde. 'Takes' good sketches in Town Planning.

As he told Professor Ball during their first meeting, achieving academic success no longer interested him, particularly after he had spent the summer vacation between the third and fourth years of the degree back in Mount Isa. As he had already completed the student program, he was able to be assigned to a work detail alongside seasoned miners of all nationalities. The experience convinced him that this was the career path he wanted to follow. By the time he came back to Melbourne he was committed to doing the bare minimum to scrape passes in all subjects.

It is not surprising then that Rob was reluctant to come home to face Margie, who was still harbouring hopes that he would concentrate his efforts on becoming a civil engineer, so he could be associated with major building enterprises in Victoria which she could identify and point out to enquiring family members. At first she accepted his excuses that he was too busy studying, but by the middle of his second year at Newman she had become so concerned about his welfare that she decided she would go to him. And she would not go alone – the whole family would pay Rob a visit at Newman.

While there had been a proliferation of privately-owned vehicles in Ballarat by the early 1960s, our family didn't have one. Margie and Barney had used a recent windfall, a bequest from an old cousin of Margie's father, to buy the Skipton St house, while her sister Kathleen bought a car. It was in that car, which Margie had borrowed, that we travelled to Melbourne one winter Sunday in 1962, despite protestations from me that I had a Physics exam the next day.

Rob was waiting for us when we arrived at Newman College. He seemed pleased to see us, giving us a tour of the College, including the room he shared with another student in the newly opened Donovan Wing. It was reasonably tidy and there was evidence of serious work being done at his desk. Our tour finished at the Walter Burley Griffin-designed chapel where Margie prayed. There was an air of relief in the car on the way back to Ballarat. Whatever Margie's worst fears had been, she had set them aside for the time being.

Mount Isa Mines

By the time Rob had completed his degree at Melbourne University, I had graduated from the School of Mines with a Diploma of Applied Chemistry and had found work as an analytical chemist, firstly with Allied Mills in Sunshine and then at Fibremakers in Bayswater. While the train service between Melbourne and Ballarat was progressively switching from steam to diesel, it was still slow and infrequent and not to be contemplated except on long weekends or Easter. Consequently, I was not at home when Rob left to take up permanent employment at Mount Isa, so I heard very little about him from Margie on our weekly trunk calls.

I imagine she wrote long flowing letters in the beautiful handwriting of which she was so proud, keeping him up to date with what his siblings were doing, including the coming marriages of myself and Jan, but I can't imagine he replied with any frequency given the attractions on offer for young single men in Mount Isa. Luckily for Margie though, he was able to return to Ballarat in December 1964, because all operations at Mount Isa Mines were at a standstill due to a dispute over pay and conditions between the mine workers and the management who, rather than enter into negotiations to reach a satisfactory agreement with them, chose to close down operations in the expectation that the workers would back down once they ran out of money. Staff pay and conditions were unaffected by the strike but, as there was little for them to do while the mine was not working, they were encouraged to take leave. Rob arrived home in time for Jan's wedding to Kevin White at St Aloysius Church in Redan, looking well-dressed and well-groomed with a girl whose name I can't remember on his arm. She was an old flame from his School of Mines days, one of the many he had visited at the Ballarat Teachers' College Hostel. He shook hands with all the uncles, flashed smiles at all the aunts and filled all the cousins in with stories of his experiences in far North Queensland, a place none of them had ever visited.

Jan's wedding was also a big success. Although she had known Kevin White for no more than six months, she had managed to persuade him to become a Catholic, which meant that the wedding ceremony could be conducted in front of the altar instead of in the sacristy, as was the custom for mixed marriages at the time. This would have been my fate six months later when I married Ken Blee, who came from a distinctly anti-Catholic family, except for the fact that the church we chose for the wedding, the Church of the Little Flower on the shores of Lake Wendouree, was undergoing extensions which had necessitated the removal of the sacristy. The priest had no alternative but to conduct the ceremony in front of the altar so the whole congregation could see us tying the knot.

Rob could not come down for my wedding, as the mine was back up and running, but I was far too preoccupied with my new married status and my own career, which was beginning to blossom in the synthetic fibre industry, to concern myself with what Rob was doing in Mount Isa. Hence, when it came to writing about Rob's life there, I had very little information to go on and the old SMB engineers were no help. They all remembered that one of their number, Tony White, had gone straight from completing his Diploma in Mechanical Engineering to Mount Isa and that he had eventually worked his way up the ranks to become the General Manager, but no one knew where he had gone after he retired except that he no longer lived in Mount Isa.

I had no better luck contacting the Human Resources Department of the current mine owners. Although the mine had been in almost continuous operation since the 1930s, there had been a number of structural changes to the way various aspects of it were managed down through the years, with Mount Isa Mines Ltd being taken over completely in more recent times. The historical employment records had long since disappeared by the time the operation of the mine had come into the hands of the Glencore Group of Companies.

After many fruitless conversations, it was suggested that I read *MIMAG*, the company magazine which was produced from 1947 to 1996. It had been digitised, and I read intently those issues that covered the period in which Rob was employed by Mount Isa Mines. I learnt a lot about the scale of the mining operation, the developments in mining technology and the importance of the mine to the economy of the country, but I could not find any mention of Rob.

Gradually though, small trickles of information opened up. I posted a request for information on the Mount Isa Historical Association Facebook page. I also wrote a profile of Rebecca Norton for a special feature the Australasian Institute of Mining and Metallurgy was running in 2018 to celebrate their 125th anniversary, together with a request that they include in their publication a request for information I could use in the biography. The Facebook page was eventually the most productive lead and I found myself communicating with a man who had worked alongside Rob for about a year during the commissioning of the K57 shaft.

He told me that Rob had initially been classed as an Award Miner and assigned to a team working on the sublevel stope development in the K73 shaft. From my reading of the MIMAG I knew that the K73 shaft was impressively large and very important to the prosperity of Mount Isa Mines, but I neglected to ask my Facebook contact what was meant by a sublevel stope and what Rob's duties would have been in its development. I have since gleaned some understanding of the process, which involves careful drilling into the wall of the ore body and blasting it so that it comes away cleanly and can be hauled to the surface leaving behind a cavity – the stope – which is stable and unlikely to collapse. Rob's ability to grasp the skills necessary to ensure the process was carried out efficiently and without danger earned him the respect of the other members of the team and recognition of his mining ability. So much so that he was soon promoted and transferred to the team responsible for overseeing the construction and commissioning of the new K57 shaft which, at the time, was the deepest manmade shaft in the world and was being fitted out with the very latest in technology, including state of the art ventilation and hauling facilities which would allow half a million tons of ore to be brought to the surface every month.

The gusto with which Rob absorbed new concepts and the approach he took to the tasks he was assigned amused the team, who compared him with a child in a lolly shop, but they also recognised his exceptional engineering brain. The team leader, who was also the chief geologist for Mount Isa Mines, nicknamed him 'Robbity Bob' – the first of the nicknames by which he was known during his time at Mount Isa.

As he had little knowledge of where Rob was employed after the commissioning of the K57 shaft was completed in late 1963, my Facebook informant took it upon himself to find other former employees who could help. What resulted was an email group consisting of old engineers and geologists who communicated with me and each other over the next few months. While their conversation veered a long way from its original purpose, they were able to put me in touch with a man who had worked with Rob once he had been seconded to the Mine Planning Department sometime in 1964. He assured me that Rob had been a valued and productive member of the team, whose role was to identify and set in motion the direction that development of the mine should follow into the future.

Rob was well-liked by everyone in the department and it was there that he acquired another of his nicknames, 'T4G Norton'. Apparently, the engineering members of the Planning Department were in the habit of taking a daily walk around the mine to inspect developments and to initiate ideas that could be worked on in the future. Invariably they had to step over or skirt around the Atlas Copco T4G Compressor, whose hose was always in the way and Rob would regularly curse the machine while giving the hose a good hard kick.

I was also able to have a telephone conversation with one of the few women employed by Mount Isa in a non-secretarial role, the cartographer for the Mine Planning Department. She described Rob as delightful and well-mannered and told me that, had she not already given her heart to someone else, she would have gladly welcomed his advances, though she didn't think she had much of a chance as he never seemed short of female companionship. While the mine workforce was almost entirely male, all the senior management had secretaries and those without a secretary took their handwritten notes to the typing pool, where the girls were usually younger and eager to be taken to the parties and other entertainments the town offered.

Eventually someone in the email group found out where Tony White had gone once he left Mount Isa – not very far as it turned out. He was living happily on the Gold Coast with Carol, the Ballarat girl he had courted throughout his School of Mines days and had married soon after graduation, and he contacted me. He hadn't heard that Rob had died, but he did know about the gender change. He told me that while their paths had often crossed during the time Rob worked in the Planning Division, they rarely saw each other socially, as he and Carol lived in the married quarters and Rob in one of the dongas – the free-standing buildings consisting of four bedrooms joined together by a long verandah, in which single male staff were accommodated.

Tony told me that he knew a couple more people who would like to contribute to the biography I was writing, so I decided to fly to Brisbane to meet them. It was good to finally communicate face to face with people who had experienced life in Mount Isa and I was able to develop a picture from listening to them talk of what it was like in the 1960s when Rob was there. One of the men had worked for a time alongside Rob in the Planning Division and knew him well, describing him as extremely capable and liked by everyone. Rob's duties had included secondments to Peko Mines at Tennant Creek and to Tasmania, where he probably observed tin mining on the west coast. He was also sent to Papua New Guinea and spent three months working on the intensive drilling program to establish if the *Here's Your Chance* deposit at MacArthur River was sufficiently large to warrant mining.

It seems that Rob gave no indication to any of the people with whom he worked that he was grappling with his gender identity. Even among the members of the Mount Isa Theatrical society it was not immediately obvious, although one of the email correspondents did remember that Rob had been spotted by the wife of the President of the Society wearing a dress. The revelation had caused a minor stir at the time because the woman almost certainly recognised the dress as coming from the wardrobe of the Society, something Rob confirmed in 1973 in his conversations with Professor Ball. No-one could remember the date on which this event had taken place, although another member of the email group felt that he bore some responsibility for Rob's actions, as it was he who had suggested that Rob join the Theatrical Society in the first place. Nobody could remember if there were any repercussions, nor were they shocked – they thought his behaviour was simply attention-seeking nonsense.

The Mount Isa Theatrical Society had been formed by a handful of people in 1954 initially to provide entertainment for the children of staff and employees at Christmas, but they built on the success of their first pantomime by staging three-act plays on a regular basis over the next few years, along with the occasional variety show. By 1964, membership stood at over 100 and they over 100 and they were ready to embark on more ambitious projects, including entering a play in the Alice Springs Festival of Drama. Although they were unplaced in the competition, they were emboldened by the venture and prepared to stage their first musical production, *South Pacific*, despite having to deal at the last moment with losing their regular performance venue, the Mission Hall, which had been absorbed by Mount Isa Mines for training purposes. After some persuasive negotiations, the proprietor of the Star Theatre was prevailed upon to provide his venue free of cost and in September 1964 the show was staged to great acclaim. Tony and Carol White were in the audience on the first night and had saved the programme, a copy of which they gave me when we met – Rob had played the part of Commander William Harrison in the production. They were also there the next year for the Society's production of *The Merry Widow*, which Rob stage managed, getting his photo in the programme along

From the program for The Merry Widow

with the Director, Chorographer and Conductor. In February 1966, the Society presented an evening of two short plays. Rob had parts in both the slightly macabre play by Harold Pinter, *Dumb Waiter*, and the Terence Rattigan comedy *Harlequinade*. The reviews posted in the *Mount Isa Mail* were quite favourable, particularly for the second play, which was described as well-paced and coordinated.

Rob was in his element! As he would tell Professor Ball in 1973, he was able to visit the Society's club rooms whenever he wanted and could access the wardrobe of costumes. He was regularly taking home dresses to wear in his room at his donga. I eventually found someone who had lived in the same donga, but when I asked him if he had ever seen Rob wearing female attire, he told me they rarely saw each other as they worked in different departments and were often on different shifts. While he was also a member of the Theatrical Society and they were on one occasion in the same production, he had no memory of Rob behaving outrageously or cross-dressing.

At the beginning of 1966, Rob was chosen to direct the most ambitious production the Society had staged to date: Ray Lawler's *Summer of the Seventeenth Doll*. He was also in charge of casting, choosing for the role of Emma a young woman who had recently moved to Mount Isa to take up a position as a draftswoman with the contract firm Theiss Brothers, where her uncle worked. The play was a wonderful success, getting rave reviews in the *Mount Isa Mail*, with readers advised, 'Don't miss this one – Doll – is first class'. Rob's skill as the Director was especially praised.

Tony and his wife Carol had also seen this play, and

were concerned that I might be influenced by some of the other people to whom I had spoken to believe that Rob was developing a less than positive reputation in the eyes of some Mount Isa residents. Anxious that the biography I was writing would paint Rob in a positive light, Tony gave me a letter he wanted me to include:

> I first met Bob Norton when we commenced a 4 year Diploma of Engineering at the Ballarat School of Mines - SMB - in 1956. Our early association was very much related to classroom discussion only and progressively moved on to general school student activities that organised a number of after hour events both in college and around the city
>
> Bob became very involved in the College events from an early stage and progressively became the leader in the development of the SMB Student Activity Report.
>
> He was a very good athlete in distance running setting himself a challenge to get to state level and I had a long held plan to become a VFL footballer and therefore we regularly trained together and became close friends and regularly discussed our future life working plans.
>
> Although Bob was not what you would call a dedicated sportsman he was a great supporter at SMB's football, basketball fixtures and the annual Ballarat Begonia Festival Parade where SMB was very successful in winning the Most Humorous award during the 4 years of Bob's involvement.
>
> At no time was his family life ever discussed, and in my case he was aware of my close association with Carol Holtan who was on his Student Activity Committee and I subsequently married 18 months after completing my Diploma. Carol remembers Bob well and like me was

most concerned when she heard of how the demons had obviously affected her working career.

Maybe we should apologise for not recognising Bob''s change of name but as Carol and I never knew him as Rebecca we will always remember him as a gentle and kind person who was always willing to help create a better living environment.

Carol and Tony White, 23 April 2019

When I read the letter in Tony's presence during our meeting in Brisbane, I was reminded of the story Jan had told me during one of her impromptu visits to my home in Winston Hills during the 1970s. According to her, Rob would volunteer to babysit for colleagues so they could have a night out with their wives. Once the children were asleep he would delve into their wardrobes trying on the wives' dresses and preening himself in front of their mirrors. Unfortunately, he was caught when one couple came home early from their date – there was an almighty blue and Rob was gone the next day.

Tony assured me that Rob had never babysat for them and he didn't know of any of their friends who had employed him as a babysitter either. I asked my other contacts and got the same answer. Everyone I talked to, however, did know about the Rodeo Ball and they wanted to tell the story even if they had not personally witnessed the event.

The Rodeo was, and still is, the event of the year in Mount Isa. Cattle men and women come from all over the Top End to take part in the festivities. Staged on the second weekend of August each year, it is organised by the

Rotary Club to raise funds for several charities across the region. In the 1960s the rodeo events took place four miles out of town at Spear Creek, where the mine had paid for the erection of fences, chutes and stands for the spectators. For those not interested in riding the bucking bulls or watching others try their luck at the sport, there was plenty of entertainment in the township itself. There were street parades, a Queen contest, concerts and a variety of performers to keep the crowd entertained well into the evening. For the staff and the distinguished guests, there was a dinner hosted by the Mine Manager which in 1966, was held in the recently opened Barkly Hotel.

In 1973, Rob told Professor Ball that the day before the rodeo he had been caught in women's clothing by some of the men who lived in the barracks, presumably miners, who had given him a beating. He was injured, but not seriously, and undaunted, he went out to rough riding events at Spear Creek dressed in a buckskin skirt and boots. At the dinner in the evening he wore what those who remembered the event described as a *pretty pink number*. Determined to be even more audacious, he then proceeded to use the women's toilets just when the Mine Manager's wife was using them.

Details about what happened next vary. Some claim that it was the Mine Manager himself who dragged Rob from the toilets. Others say that it was the Regional Manager for Northern Queensland, who was also in charge of the Planning Division in which Rob worked, who was sent in to get him out. Either way, he was ousted from the hotel and the story was all over Mount Isa by the morning. Whether he was sacked on the spot or hauled before the management in the days afterwards is a matter of some dispute. My informants weren't interested in that part of the story. In any case, his time at Mount Isa was at an end.

Mia

I was on the other side of the world on the day Rebecca died. As had been my practice whenever I was away from Ballarat for any length of time, I had given all Rebecca's important papers to my daughter Emma, including instructions that she was to act on my behalf. Invariably she would return them to me when I arrived home. But not on 17 August 2017.

It was midnight where I was staying in Cornwell when she rang me to tell me that the charge sister at Kirralee Nursing Home had rung her to tell her that Rebecca was dying. As it would be morning before I could make arrangements to fly home, I let my mind wander over the events of her life I knew about and speculated on all that I didn't know. To help the process I wrote, not very coherently at first, but by the time Emma rang to tell me she had arranged a flight for me, I had the makings of an obituary notice on my iPad. We agreed I should post it on Facebook. I didn't know if Rebecca was known on Facebook, but there were plenty of people who knew me and the bond that existed between us.

I copied what I had written and posted:

> Vale Rebecca Michelle Norton.
>
> Born Robert Michael Norton on 30 December 1940 in Ballarat to Marge and Barney Norton, her childhood and adolescence was one of achievement winning her scholarships to study mining and civil engineering at the School of Mines in Ballarat and at Melbourne University. Her mining career took her all over Australia and beyond both as Robert and Rebecca and she was renowned through the industry, sometimes for her colourful dresses and flamboyant hats.
>
> Her personal life was not so straightforward. Making the decision to change her gender was difficult and it left her isolated from many of those she held dear, but for those of us who knew her well before illness dominated her, she was a font of great knowledge and a wonderful raconteur. There will never be another like her.

Some weeks later an old friend told me that he had reposted the obituary on a trans site to which he belonged and had received some replies. One was from a woman called Mia who wanted to get in touch with me and I emailed her. She replied with the words, 'Robert Michael Norton was my father'.

I rang her.

Mia had been born in Mount Isa in November 1966. She and her mother had left Mt Isa a few weeks after her birth and she had never been back, but she had never stopped asking who her father was. It was not until she turned fifteen that her mother finally gave her his name. She had been searching for him ever since without success, because by then Robert Michael Norton did not exist.

She told me that her mother was the person Rob had

cast as Emma in *The Summer of the Seventeenth Doll* and that they had a brief affair which lasted until she told him she was pregnant. I spoke with Mia's mother who confirmed her story. While Rob's prowess as a lover left a lot to be desired, especially as he had armed himself with copious quantities of booze before the event, and seemed to have difficulty reaching a climax, she was delighted that he had made her pregnant, as she had been told by doctors that she would never conceive. She had been badly damaged in an accident when she was six.

In 1973, Rob admitted to Professor Ball, when asked if he had ever had children, that he had been a virgin until he was twenty-six, and that he had been accused of making a girl pregnant shortly afterwards. Encouraged by the advice of the blokes in the barracks, however, he decided that the evidence was inconclusive and he could deny responsibility. He was no longer in Mount Isa when Mia was born, so he almost certainly did not receive the letter her mother sent to him. Mia offered to take a DNA test to prove she was Rob's daughter, but in the meantime, she sent photos of herself and her children. When they arrived, I decided there was no need for the test. The resemblances were remarkable. Mia was Margie and Barney's first grandchild.

The Mine Manager's Ticket

In the folder of certificates I had found on the bookshelf of Rebecca's apartment after she had gone into care in 2012 were her Mine Manager's certificates, one issued by the Queensland Department of Mines and the other by the Victorian Mines Department. I realised these must have been like gold to her, as she would be unlikely to be able to apply for positions of authority in any mine in Australia without them after she left Mount Isa. I remembered them when I began searching for details about her mining career and decided I had to find out how and when she had been awarded them.

I telephoned the Queensland Department of Mines and talked to the archivist, who was only too happy to search the departmental archives provided I could demonstrate a legitimate need for the information I requested. Once again, I gathered up birth and death certificates, the no longer valid Power of Attorney and a brief explanation of the project I was undertaking. Within a week I had all the information I needed. It had apparently long been the practice of the Queensland Department of Mines to conduct an annual examination for the First Class Metalliferous Mine Managers Certificate of Competency, generally known in the industry as a Mine Manager's Ticket. Details and application forms were sent out to all substantial mines in Queensland along with the list of prerequisites needed and the date and place where the examination could be taken.

Although this information had almost certainly been posted on multiple notice boards across various offices of Mount Isa Mines, Rob had either not noticed, or had put off doing anything about it until after the closing date for applications. He then scribbled off a rushed request on a scrappy piece of paper to the Queensland Department of Mines asking to be allowed to take the examination. The Directors were unimpressed by the tardiness of his application and the manner in which they had received it, and returned the note to him as he had overlooked signing it. He had also neglected to provide proof of his eligibility to apply for the opportunity to take the examinations in the form of his academic record. He wrote back immediately on proper writing paper, begging the Directors' forgiveness and once again asking to be allowed to take the examinations, this time including copies of his two School of Mines diplomas and his degree from Melbourne University. They accepted his apology grudgingly, notifying the Inspector of Mines that Rob would be a candidate for the examination on December 8 1965 at the Mount Isa Court House.

From the Department of Mines Archives I was sent a sheaf of papers, including the original scribbled note and the terse reply from the Directors. The archivist also sent me a copy of the exam questionnaire and Rob's hand-written exam paper. All questions were answered in detail and very neatly – there were no crossings out or anything that would indicate hesitancy. He passed with flying colours, but he still had to satisfy the Directors as to his First Aid Certificate, which was a condition of holding a Mine Manager's ticket. A copy of that certificate was also in the archives, as was the First Class Metalliferous Mine Managers Certificate No 3012 which had been issued on 18th February 1966. With this piece of paper, he could be employed as a Mine Manager in Queensland and the Northern Territory in particular, but it was also recognised in most places in Australia, which was very fortunate, as it would be needed before another year was out.

It seems that Rob didn't immediately start looking for a job, deciding instead to head for Sydney because, as he told Professor Ball, he had convinced himself that he had what it took to perform in the cabaret act *Les Girls* which had been entertaining packed houses in Kings Cross since 1963. Although he wasn't offered a part in the cabaret, he did strike up an acquaintance with some of the cast, which he was able to rekindle when both he and a second troupe of *Les Girls* moved to the Gold Coast at the beginning of 1967.

The Gold Coast was fast becoming the *in* destination for Australians looking for some of the American style excitement they were watching on their televisions. The long sandy beaches, nightclubs and scantily clad Meter Maids were particularly attractive to people anxious to escape the cold wet winters of Southern Australia. *Les Girls*, which presented their cabaret at the Coolangatta Hotel, provided an additional thrill for the holiday makers with their exotic appearance, fabulous costuming and professional performances. While Rob still didn't get a stage role with the troupe, he was able to maintain his friendship with the cast while at the same time managing a sand dredging operation on Stradbroke Island.

The presence in the beach sands of northern New South Wales of extractable quantities of Rutile and Zircon had been known for some years, but until the rapid development in military hardware during and following World War II, there was little interest in extracting them until the racing magnate Jack Forster, who owned a large slice of the north coast of New South Wales, saw the possibility that demand would skyrocket following the Korean War and the outbreak of tensions in Indochina. He employed teams of men to dig up, wash, bag and store the black ore in anticipation of making a fortune from its sale to munitions factories that realised its potential in building new and more lethal armaments that would be needed if the Cold War turned deadly.

By the time Rob was employed to manage the Stradbroke Island division of Jack Forster's dredging company Curzon XL, dredges had replaced men with shovels and the primitive washing techniques that had been in use previously. The whole operation of washing and extraction could be carried out in situ, with the cleaned sand being redeposited on the beach from which it had come. While less disastrous to the contours of the coast, the dredges destroyed the marine flora and fauna in their paths, not that Rob was ever very concerned about the damage mining did to the environment. He almost certainly viewed the whole process as a great comedown from the excitement of having been involved in mining in one of the deepest underground mines in the world at the time. The only benefit was that he could spend his evenings with his friends at *Les Girls*. He did enough to satisfy his employers at Curzon XL, gaining promotion from Site Manager at Stradbroke Island to being appointed Manager of the entire sand mining operation on both sides of the Queensland/New South Wales border. This meant a pay rise and the use of a car to get between the various sites.

I don't know when Margie and Barney became aware that Rob was no longer at Mount Isa Mines because at about the same time they had undergone the most momentous upheaval of their lives, caused in the first instance by injuries Barney had received as a result of a collision he had been involved in while delivering parcels around Ballarat for Myer. Although he made a full recovery, he was reluctant to return to driving for his living, but jobs for unskilled or semi-skilled middle-aged men in Ballarat were almost non-existent. He was impressed by what I had told him about Fibremakers which, being heavily protected by trade tariffs at the time, had a monopoly on the production of synthetic fibres in Australia, and was constantly building its workforce.

Before he could contemplate taking a job there as a storeman, however, he and Margie had to sell the house they had lived in since they were married and had owned since Margie was left a bequest by an old cousin of her father. They then had to find a find a house in Melbourne and a school for Louise. Liz remained in Ballarat as a boarder at Sacred Heart College until she completed Year Twelve. Rob must have eventually caught up with the details of the house they had bought in Box Hill and let them know he was living at Broadbeach while managing a sand mining company. I expect I found out about the same time, but whether Margie was able to see this development in her son's career in a positive light I don't know. Broadbeach was at least in a settled part of south Queensland and was accessible by road from Melbourne. She must have been sufficiently confident that Rob had matured into a sensible young businessman that she arranged to send Liz and Louise up to stay with him during one school holiday. They saw little of him, the wife of one of his employees being deputised to attend to their needs. They spent their days window shopping and sitting on the beach reading, but he did take them for one long walk along the sand to demonstrate to them how the rare earths could be detected before any dredging commenced. Apparently, there is a squeaking sound under the feet if the rare earths are present even in microscopic quantities.

He didn't take his sisters to *Les Girls*, but he did invite a Mount Isa couple with whom he had been friends during his time in the Theatrical Society to dinner and a show at the cabaret. According to those I met in Brisbane, he asked the cast of the show to join their table for after dinner drinks. It wasn't until the couple returned to Mount Isa that they were told that the women whose performance they had enjoyed so much were in fact men in drag. Rob had not enlightened them, nor did they notice any change in his appearance, even though he admitted in one of his interviews with Professor Ball that he had begun taking estrogen tablets around this time to enhance his breasts. They had been supplied to him by some of his friends at

Les Girls who had access to the drugs, which were imported illegally from America. While not all members of the troupe, including their Master of Ceremonies Peter Mozelle, interviewed for the National Library of Australia Oral History Project, were anxious to portray themselves as women, some were determined to feminise their bodies by drug taking and breast enhancement surgery. Some of the troupe were even contemplating radical gender surgery, which could only be performed clandestinely in Australia at the time. Mozelle assured the interviewer that he had no desire to be anything other than a female impersonator.

Rob didn't take me to *Les Girls* either when I met him in Brisbane early in 1968. I had been sent there to attend a conference on Spectroscopy at Queensland University because I had recently persuaded Fibremakers to purchase an atomic absorption spectrometer, to enable the company to measure the effectiveness of the cleaning process I had devised for the melting pots used to extrude polymer. It was quite a breakthrough at the time, as the cleaning process reduced the amount of polymer wasted each time a new pot was inserted into the line. But Rob didn't want to know anything about it. He met me, as arranged by Margie, outside the student residences of the University at the finish of the conference and drove me to Broadbeach, where we stopped briefly at the house he was renting before going to a pub for a beer. He talked about dredging and other mining issues and showed no interest in my research before delivering me to the airport. I remember being annoyed and somewhat surprised by his very scruffy appearance, but little else.

During this time Rob managed to maintain an infrequent correspondence with Margie that gave no hint of any trauma in his life. Job changes were simply a means of gaining experience in his chosen field, so when she and Barney and Louise set off to visit him a few months after I had seen him, they had no inkling that there was anything wrong. By that stage he had moved to Kempsey on the northern New South Wales coast, ostensibly because, according to him, he needed to be closer to the Curzon XL dredges on the New South Wales side of the border. They stayed in a nearby motel and saw about as much of him as Liz and Louise had on the Gold Coast. It is quite possible that he was no longer employed by Curzon XL.

When asked to talk about his employment history by Professor Ball in 1973, Rob told him that he left Curzon XL early in 1968 because the Board of Directors could not be trusted, but he did not say why. It is also possible that while he was showing Margie and Barney around he was living in a quasi-lesbian relationship with a woman called Gil. She had been married and had four children, although they were probably not living with her. He told the Professor that he got into the relationship because he needed a woman to help him perfect his transvestism, and things got out of hand. He left her to take up work in the Northern Territory, but went back to see her during a break from work in the Territory in an effort to repair their relationship. By then, though, she had decided she no longer wanted a partnership with a man masquerading as a woman.

Hatches Creek

I can't remember how or when I found out that Rob was no longer beach sand mining in Queensland and Northern New South Wales. It is possible, I suppose, that he had already resigned from Curzon XL or been sacked when he took me to the airport after my brief visit to Brisbane. I presume he told Margie that he was moving to a place called Hatches Creek in the Northern Territory, almost certainly sending her and Barney on a search among the old school atlases still in the house to find exactly where this place was. They would have located it, if it was marked, on the edge of the Tanami Desert about half way between Darwin and Alice Springs, but they had to wait until he bothered to contact them again before they could glean his reasons for moving there.

Although he almost certainly did not mention gold in his next communication with her, Margie convinced herself that it was gold he was mining out there in the desert because she had been raised in the gold mining city of Ballarat, where three generations of her family had lived and prospered. By the time relatives began asking her where Rob was and what he was doing, she had convinced herself that not only would he be mining gold, but that he had bought the mine as well.

I didn't question what she told me, as I had more important issues to deal with – I was pregnant. Knowing the policy of British Nylon Spinners, who owned Fibremakers, towards the employment of married women, I had successfully hidden the fact under my white lab coat for nearly four months, but when one of the men in suits was made aware of my situation, probably from the gossip around the tea trolley, I was called into the office of the departmental head and given my marching orders. It didn't matter that I was involved in ongoing research into antistatic finishes so necessary for the production of synthetic fibres and I still had my notes to collate, the offence I was causing to the eyes of the men in suits took precedence. I was dismissed and then had to face the displeasure of my husband Ken Blee, who was relying on my income to help make the payments on our mortgage. He hadn't factored in any interruption due to the arrival of children, which he hoped would be delayed for years to come. While he had no choice but to accept the inevitable, he remained a reluctant parent throughout our marriage.

The arrival of her first legitimate granddaughter in March 1969 was enough to temporarily distract Margie from her concerns about Rob, but after months of waiting for letters which didn't come, her anxieties were accumulating. She decided that she and Barney would have to find Hatches Creek and personally check on his wellbeing. Whether Barney offered any resistance to this venture I don't know, but having never driven outside Victoria except during his time in the Civil Construction Corps, this was an enormous undertaking for him and his small four-cylinder Ford.

Barney drove, with Margie in the passenger seat, as she had never learned to drive, up through western New South Wales to Alice Springs, where they stopped for a couple of days before heading up the Stuart Highway to Hatches Creek. Along the way they must have stopped at every Catholic Church they passed as photos of them, inside and out, filled the small photo album Margie produced once she was safely home again in Box Hill. While she would not normally find anything worth photographing about churches of other denominations, she did include in the album photos of the John Flynn Memorial Church in Alice Springs because it was a landmark she had read about. After finding Rob at Hatches Creek, there were more photos of the Catholic Churches they visited in Darwin.

Barney took slides which I don't recall seeing at the time. He must have given them to Rob at some stage because I found them, along with the folder of certificates, when I was cleaning up. Although we no longer had a projector with which to view them, Emma was able to transfer the images to her computer. Among them were some of Hatches Creek, but they told me little about the mine and Rob's living conditions. There were a couple of newish square buildings which looked like they could accommodate workers, a collection of machinery strewn about and a poppet head. There was one slide of Rob looking decidedly scruffy in dirty jeans and shirt.

Where Barney and Margie stayed while they were at Hatches Creek I have no idea, but I doubt that there was any suitable accommodation, and the conditions of the camp would have had Margie turning up her nose at them. She didn't contribute any information about Rob's employees, most of whom, I discovered many years later, were criminals with warrants on their heads who chose to live and work out of sight of the constabulary. Nor did Margie mention the dogs which inhabited the camp. Mostly part dingo, they were kept in check by a matriarch called Delia who was a particular favourite of Rob's, and engendered in him a great love of dogs in later life, particularly if they had a touch of dingo in their makeup.

Once home Margie said little about the trip. She was relieved when they were finally on the east coast of the continent and travelling down the highway to Victoria. I took in little of what she had to say at the time, as I had other things on my mind, such as how I was going to cope with the arrival of another child less than twelve months after the first.

When I began writing about this chapter of Rebecca's life, I had only a handful of poor-quality photos and slides, and a handful of stories about Delia and her pups she was willing to share with me during our late afternoon drinking sessions in her little apartment in Canadian, the suburb adjacent to Ballarat East. The only other story she told me related to her good citizen decision to allow some of her workforce to join in the search for a missing tourist in the Tanami desert. Unfortunately, they were recognised by the policemen leading the search and were arrested on outstanding warrants. This episode undoubtedly contributed to the poor opinion of the police she harboured for the rest of her life.

The only other information Rebecca left me about Hatches Creek was a brief description of her duties in one of the numerous curriculum vitae she wrote in the 1990s. Written in her cryptic style her duties included:

> Establishment and production, including mill (Wo, Bi). This was a narrow vein operation, dip 45 degrees. Six satellite mines reopened for feasibility (two for minor production) and six remote test shafts sunk for turquoise and phosphate at Amaroo, 100km south.

At least I knew that gold was not the desired product, and the mine site was owned by Northern Territory Minerals, not Rob, who was employed to manage the mining for Wolfram and Bismuth as well as turquoise and phosphate. In an effort to find more information about the mining company and its operations at Hatches Creek, I contacted the Northern Australian Department of Mines. Although they had never heard of Robert or Rebecca Norton, they could tell me a considerable amount about mining around the Tanami Desert. They sent the precise directions for Hatches Creek – 336 kilometres northeast of Alice Springs and 270 kilometres south east of Tennant Creek Hatches – and they provided information about its history. The region has been mined intermittently since the beginning of the 20th century, initially for gold, but by the beginning of World War I, for Wolfram, the ore from which tungsten is obtained. When the price of tungsten dropped post-war the place was abandoned, only to be revived during World War II. To boost production then, the Government dispatched 500 indentured Chinese labourers who had been evacuated from the British Phosphate Commission operations on Nauru, upsetting the local miners who eventually had to be compensated. As the price of tungsten fell again after 1945, many of the mines were abandoned and the camp where the Chinese had lived was bulldozed. The living conditions for the Australian miners was little better. The only substantial building in the area was the Police Station, which was destroyed by fire in 1961.

Renewed interest in the Wolfram deposits at Hatches Creek came with the escalation of hostilities in Indochina. In February 1968, a new company declared an interest in reopening one of the existing mines owned by Pioneer Mines NL, and commenced building a camp for the workers. There is no way of knowing how Rob came to hear about the pending operation, but it seems that he was employed almost immediately and by the time Margie and Barney visited, the mine and the mill were both up and running and he was exploring the country around Amaroo, 100 kilometres south of Hatches Creek, for turquoise.

Rob arrived back in Melbourne unannounced at the end of February 1970 while I was in hospital following the birth of my son Geoffrey. Although Margie was undoubtedly pleased to see him looking clean, healthy and well-groomed she could not offer him a bed, as Liz and Louise were still living at home and she had my daughter Emma, who was about to have her first birthday, staying with her. As she palmed him off to Jan, who had her own apartment in Toorak, she managed to put a favourable spin on his departure from Hatches Creek – he was moving on to greener pastures.

He almost certainly didn't tell her that he had been fired because he was caught wearing women's clothing in a public place in Adelaide. He told Professor Ball that he had taken some leave towards the end of 1969, but had the misfortune to run into one of the Directors of NT Minerals at the races, dressed as he was in his best race-going attire. He was instantly dismissed, but he didn't come to Melbourne immediately. Instead he flew to Brisbane because he wanted help to break his addiction to phenobarbitone, which had started when he was doing shift work in Mount Isa. He had initially been prescribed Amatal to help him deal with his inability to sleep during the day, but when the prescription ran out he took to using phenobarbitone, which he purchased on the black market. Through his *Les Girls* friends he had heard of a doctor who could treat him, no questions asked.

The doctor, who had his practice in Wickham Terrace in Brisbane, did more than treat people with drug dependencies. His clientele included people wanting help with changing their body shape. Consequently, Rob was admitted to St Andrews Hospital where, while he dealt with the symptoms of drug withdrawal, he also had insulin injections directly into his breasts to encourage augmentation. Although the practice was not approved or even recommended by the medical profession, it was common among prostitutes and female impersonators at the time.

While Margie probably didn't notice any difference in Rob's breast profile, Jan almost certainly did although it is hard to know how much Jan knew about Rob's desire to live as a woman at this time. She was living a single life in Toorak by then, having left Myer to join a consultancy firm providing advice and programming for companies embarking on what was then breakthrough computer technology. She had been long separated from Kevin, although she retained his surname of White and stayed legally married to him until no fault divorce became law in 1975. As a consultant she was earning considerably more than she had as a secretary. She had money to burn, along with a personality which attracted anyone who wanted to party. Champagne and cigarettes smoked through long cigarette holders were a common sight at her apartment in Toorak.

Whether Rob experimented with dressing up in Jan's clothes – they were the same height – or she taught him more about wearing make-up, I don't know. I also don't know when he left Toorak to go north to work again. My conversations with Margie at the time revolved around babies and their needs, not the welfare of my siblings.

A Mining Gypsy

With a babe in arms, another child not yet walking and a husband sulking because he did not have my undivided attention, I had no time to concern myself with Rob's issues. He did not make the effort to come out to Bayswater, where we had settled, and I had no desire to drive in to the inner suburbs, even though I had the wheels to do so. Ken and I had acquired an ancient Valiant station wagon with no seat belts and nothing with which I could strap the baby's bassinet to the back seat.

As Margie was working in the HCF Medical Benefits office in Melbourne at the time, she and Barney visited every Saturday, Margie to cuddle the baby and play with Emma, and Barney to potter around our not very well-kept garden, but they rarely mentioned Rob or what he was doing, except on one occasion telling me that he had applied to join the Australian Antarctic Expedition. I have to assume that he was unsuccessful, as the matter was never mentioned again. Perhaps the people doing the selections were aware of rumours about Rob's gender issues at the time. By the middle of 1970, it became apparent that Rob was no longer in Melbourne, but I didn't ask where he had gone. I doubt Margie knew anyway.

I didn't find out until I started reading through the

curriculum vitae after Rob had died. Not that they were initially much use. Written long after this period of Rob's life, during which he applied for and took jobs that were short-term and seemed invariably to have ended abruptly, they were full of contradictions and discrepancies about the order in which he took mining jobs and left them again. Dates and places didn't line up. In one of them he wrote that in the summer of 1969/70 he had been in charge of the 'exploration, support and development at one gold and several old copper mines' for Newmetal at Mt Lindsay, a heavily prospected region of North Queensland west of Mount Isa, which was impossible because he was in hospital in Brisbane over the same period and then in Melbourne by late February 1970.

Attached to most of the curriculum vitae was a list of referees, but by the time I was trying to contact them, most had either moved location and telephone number, or had passed away. I was close to giving up on this avenue of research when one of the numbers I rang was answered by a man who knew Rob well. Not only had he worked with Rob in Mount Isa, but he could tell me where he went after he left Melbourne in the winter of 1970. He had headed to far North Queensland to a place called Gunpowder, 110 km north of Mount Isa. My contact remembered working with him and the draftswoman from the Planning Division at Mount Isa, who had been forced to find alternative employment when she married, due to the Mount Isa Mines policy of not employing married women in non-secretarial roles. The company at Gunpowder was run by VAM Limited and was headed by the man who had previously been Mount Isa's Regional Manager for

Northern Queensland. He was also the person who had taken Rob from the Barkly Hotel toilets on the night of that infamous ball.

While the prospect of returning to underground copper mining in a field as rich as the vast Mammoth deposit at Gunpowder would have been exciting for Rob, he had to contend with fitting into a community which was largely made up of men he had worked with in Mount Isa. They would all have known about his cross-dressing escapades and the reasons for his dismissal. Not that my informant would admit to any tensions in the company in this regard, but the fact that Rob was gone from Gunpowder within a few months would suggest that his notoriety presented difficulties among some sections of the staff.

By late September 1970 I was aware that Rob was in Kempsey in Northern New South Wales, because Margie and Barney were again planning the long drive up there to visit him. I have to assume that he had been in contact with them after he left Gunpowder. Perhaps he even invited them to visit although, given the claims he made on one of the curriculum vitae, it is hard to imagine he could spare much time for them. He claimed to be managing three different mine sites at the same time. All were existing operations which needed to be brought back into production. This meant extending, and in some cases widening, mine shafts and re-instating the associated mills. At Munga Creek he was mining antimony in a narrow seam. At a nearby mine called Abaleen there was both an underground mine and an open cut process where both Wolfram and tin were being mined. At the same time, he had responsibility for sapphire mining in the same region.

When they returned from Kempsey, Margie and Barney were happy to show off the snaps they had taken – more Catholic Churches, along with the outsides of the motels they had stayed in and some beach shots, but there were none of Rob or of the mines he was supposedly managing. They were equally unforthcoming about how well or happy he was. Not that I asked. It would appear though, according to what he told Professor Ball, that he was gone from Kempsey not long after their visit, because the conditions under which he had been expected to work he found intolerable due to the erratic behaviour of the mine owner.

His contract was terminated and he was once again out of work, this time for about five months, during which time he was in Sydney because he wanted to see a doctor who would give him injections of the estrogen hormone Stilboestrol to enhance the size of his breasts. He continued this treatment in both injection and tablet form for a few months and was pleased with the improvement in body shape as well as in his hair and skin texture, which he claimed gave him greater overall relaxation and poise. He had commenced facial epilation but he was fast running out of money. Knowing that he would be unlikely to get any engineering work in Sydney, he became a rigger on a building site. How successful he was at this very manual work he didn't say. He told Ball that he left after three months because a professional job became available, working as a metallurgist for New Zealand Steel Limited south of Auckland, which was extracting iron from the black beach sands on the west coast of the North Island.

Accepting such a position would have been quite a

comedown for Rob, who viewed metallurgists and applied chemists as well down the employment hierarchy on his scale of importance. Their only purpose in life was to assay the minerals once the engineers had done all the work of extracting the ore and bringing it to the surface where it could be smelted into useful product. It is not surprising that he was soon at loggerheads with mine management over the tasks he was being asked to perform and was once again out of work. While he had found a good supply of estrogen in Auckland, which was cheaper than any he could buy in Sydney, he must have considered his job prospects were better in New South Wales, because the man who had told me about the Gunpowder mine in North Queensland encountered him back in Kempsey towards the end of 1971.

Rob was again managing another small mine, but my informant could not remember the details except that he was no longer being discreet about his cross-dressing and had been the victim of much abuse and a fair amount of 'poofter' bashing at the hands of the young males of the town. Despite the risks to himself he insisted on wearing a dress, high heel shoes and a handbag when they went to dinner at the local pub, running the gauntlet of the wolf whistles from the bar as they made their way to the restaurant area, which made for an uncomfortable evening. On the way back to Rob's accommodation one night, a police car pulled up behind them at an intersection and Rob panicked, diving under the dashboard in an effort to make himself invisible. His story reminded me of similar experiences driving Rob around Ballarat decades later.

I am almost sure that Margie and Barney did not know

about Auckland or that Rob was back in Kempsey, and when Margie's letters began returning unopened, they were very worried. I arrived at their house one morning to find them quite distressed. They had begun opening mail addressed to Rob and discovered to their shock that he had paid no income tax for some years, probably since he had left Mount Isa, and the Australian Taxation Office was instituting proceedings against him. Barney had rung and made an appointment for himself and Margie to see someone in the Melbourne office of the ATO so they could discuss what options were available to them to prevent Rob from being prosecuted. Reluctantly, Margie told me they had agreed to take on the tax debt and had entered into an arrangement to pay it off over several years. Even when they finally located Rob, they did not tell him what they had done. By then he was in Thailand.

Outwardly, Margie took the news that he was going to Thailand as an indication that his ability as a mining engineer was being recognised by major international companies. Inwardly though, she and Barney were frightened. Like most Australians at the time, they had been watching the unfolding story of the war in Vietnam on their televisions each night, and were well aware of the role Thailand was playing in providing bases from which American aircraft could carry out bombing raids on Vietnam, Laos and Cambodia. They also knew that Thailand was the destination for thousands of American and Allied troops on rest and recuperation leave, and bars, brothels and night clubs of all descriptions had sprung up in cities like Bangkok to cater for the cashed-up soldiers.

Rob had given them the name of the company he said had employed him to manage their fluorspar mines. According to one of his curriculum vitae it was called Leighton Paitan Joint Venture, trading under Petchbury Mining Limited, with offices in Pethchaburi Road in Bangkok. Although mining of fluorspar continues to this day in Thailand, that particular company no longer exists, so there was no possibility of confirming Rob's employment. He did give Margie and Barney an address of an apartment he said he would be using whenever he was in Bangkok, but he expected to be spending most of his time at the mine sites, which were all in the north west of the country around Chiang Mai and Chiang Rai.

Fluorspar has been mined for centuries in this region for gemstones and for slabs of the mineral suitable for carving images of deities, principally the Buddha, but it is also a valuable source of fluorine, which has uses in a wide variety of chemical, metallurgical and ceramic processes as well as for the manufacture of lenses for microscopes, telescopes and cameras. Commercial mining on a large scale began in about 1960 and was centred around the northern provinces of Lamphun, Chiangmai, Lampang, and Mae Hong Son. By the early 1970s, Thailand was one of the world's leading producers of fluorite. In 1971, a new venture at the Da Mok Mine in the Chiang Rai district began, possibly owned or managed by Petchbury Mining Limited.

Rob told Professor Ball he lasted three months with this company, and he was back in Bangkok to receive a letter from Margie telling him that her cousin Marion would pay him a visit during a stopover of the cruise ship on which she was travelling. I don't know whether she and her husband were met by Rob off the ship or they found their own way to his apartment, but he certainly entertained them to tea, although he had never met them before.

Marion often featured in Margie's stories as we were growing up. They were the same age, but could never be called friends. Margie resented the fact that Marion's parents, having only two daughters, were able to indulge them with beautiful clothes and could take them on outings that the ten O'Farrell children could only dream of. After they both married, the animosity between them only increased. Marion's husband was a farmer of German descent from the Hahndorf region of South Australia, whereas Barney continued until long after I had left home to be a delivery driver. Margie could at least boast in the long but infrequent telephone conversations they had that she had produced five fine children, the oldest of whom was exceptional – Marion had no children. It was presumably in one such telephone conversation that Marion boasted about taking a cruise on an ocean liner that stopped in Bangkok, and Margie gave her Rob's address.

Marion had quite a reputation as a snoop – she seemed devoted to getting to the bottom of all the family secrets. She investigated the lengthy absences of various female cousins, aunts and nieces to discover if they had been pregnant at the time of their disappearance. She managed to track down where some of them had spent their confinement and what had happened to their offspring. She even tried to make contact with adoptive parents and she passed on this knowledge to Margie and all the other cousins who were on her telephone list. She knew who drank too much, who gambled, and who was unfaithful to his wife and she also knew what Rob had been up to in Thailand, or thought she did.

When she returned to Australia, she told another cousin that she had proof that Rob had a girlfriend with whom he was sharing the apartment in Bangkok. She had a good snoop around, finding women's clothing in the wardrobe and lots of makeup in the bathroom cupboard. It didn't dawn on her that both the clothes and the makeup were for Rob's personal use. Nor would she have known about the Thai ambivalence about gender and the existence of what has euphemistically been called the third gender, the 'ladyboys' or *kathoeys*, who dress as women.

With the proliferation of nightclubs and cabarets in Bangkok and other tourist spots like Chiang Mai, the *kathoey* found themselves in demand and the more feminine they could make themselves appear, the better their chances of earning a living. As a result, a medical industry grew up around them, offering hormone therapy and other services. In 1972 when Rob arrived in Thailand, these clinics were not yet offering transgender reassignment but were increasingly attracting wealthy clients from America and Europe who were undergoing a range of body modifications in luxurious hotel-style private hospitals. Rob of course could not afford such luxury. He told Professor Ball that he got some work in a nightclub show and he also started a relationship with a Major in the United States Airforce which lasted for about six weeks. After they broke up, he again had hormone injections in his breasts and face.

In the meantime, Margie and Barney were becoming increasingly alarmed by stories they were seeing on television about escalating conflict in the regions around Chiang Mai and Chiang Rai as the neighbouring Burmese military regime harassed, tortured and displaced the ethnic minorities inside their border who had been fighting for an independent homeland since the end of British occupation in 1949. With nowhere else to go, refugees crossed the border into Thailand, only to be pushed back by the Thai authorities. When Margie's letters to Rob were once again returned unanswered, they convinced themselves that he had come to harm in one of these skirmishes and they sought the help of the Department of Foreign Affairs. The correspondence they received in return has long since been lost, but presumably they were reassured that no Australians had been caught up in the conflict. Whether anyone from the Australian Embassy in Thailand was able to track Rob down is also unknown, but if they did they would probably have told him to get in contact with his parents, which he didn't.

Instead, he turned up in Box Hill in March 1973 while Margie and Barney were away on holiday down on the Gippsland Lakes. Liz and Louise found him in the backyard of the family home feeding women's dresses from a suitcase into Barney's incinerator. He had apparently planned to stay, but such was the reaction of the girls that he thought better of it and packed up his suitcase and left, but not before giving them some contact details and getting them to promise not to tell Margie and Barney that they had seen him. He also told them that he had had surgery and was now a woman.

They didn't try to contact Margie and Barney – instead they rang me. They wanted me to go and talk to him, but I was two weeks away from giving birth to my third child by Caesarean Section and was in no fit state to be driving into South Melbourne, where he told them he was living, so I prevailed on my husband to go in my stead. They met in a pub in South Melbourne, Rob dressed in male attire, although he did have shoulder length hair, something that was not so unusual for the time. He told Ken he had a place to live and a job sewing curtains in a curtain factory and that he had already undergone surgery to become a woman. He had changed his name from Robert to Rebecca and no amount of pleading by the family was going to change the situation.

By the time my son Phillip was born on April 17 1973, Margie had made decisions which would affect the family for the rest of Rob's life. I don't know whether she had met with him, but she had talked with the Parish Priest, who had offered his prayers and nothing else. She decided that we were not to talk about Rob and what he had done. Nor was he allowed to attend any family gathering, especially extended family celebrations and funerals, at which Margie would provide the standard explanation for his absence, which was to be told to any pesky aunt, uncle or cousin who had the temerity to ask 'Where's Rob?'

To my shame, I voiced no resistance to this edict – I was too engrossed in my own rapidly changing world at the time. Before I left hospital after Phillip's birth, Ken had informed me that Unilever, who owned Rosella Foods where he had been employed as an analytical chemist for some years, was transferring him to Head Office in

Sydney. During the next six weeks we had to sell our home in Bayswater and purchase another, at twice the price, in the Winston Hills district in Sydney. Then, while Ken began acclimatising himself to working in the company headquarters at Circular Quay, I had to pack up three small children, the dog and our belongings for transfer to a city I knew nothing about and had only visited once. I had no time to consider Rob's situation or the implications of Margie's decisions.

Becoming Rebecca

The place to which Ken and I moved during the winter of 1973 was as far removed from the picture postcard views of Sydney's wide sandy beaches as possible. Nor was Winston Hills anywhere near the sleazy attractions of places like Kings Cross that I occasionally read about as I flipped through magazines at the hairdressers with something of a guilty conscience, knowing that what I was seeing and reading was almost certainly forbidden for good Catholics like me to even know about. I had grown up listening to sermons by supposedly celibate priests harping on about the dangers of unnatural acts and the punishments God would bring down on those who engaged in them, never once hearing an explanation as to what constituted an unnatural act. Just speaking about them was a sin, as was the word 'sex' and, as I was to find out when I was eleven years old, the word 'pregnant'. After the belting Sister Mercy gave me for talking dirty, she told me that I should say that my mother was 'in the family way'.

According to the education provided in Catholic schools, sexual relations could only take place between a man and a woman provided they were married in the eyes of God at the time. All other relationships were sinful and those between people of the same gender were also illegal, but as no explanations were given as to what those relationships entailed, the instruction left a lot to be desired. The words 'homosexual' and 'lesbian' were never used. Hence, they were not part of my vocabulary until well after I was confronted with Rebecca's decision to change gender.

Not that I could educate myself about what the gender change she was planning entailed. It would be another thirty years before information searches of this nature were a mere click of a mouse away, and there was no library in Winston Hills. In fact, streets full of newly erected houses were the only buildings of any substance in Winston Hills. I presume that there was a library in Parramatta, which was the nearest population centre of note, but with a babe in arms and two pre-schoolers in tow, undertaking any sort of information search was out of the question. It was easier to consign Rebecca's situation to the back of my mind and concentrate my time and energy on establishing a home for myself, my husband and our three children in the largely foreign state of New South Wales.

I wasn't entirely cut off from everything I had known before the move, as Margie once again had an excuse to display her magnificent handwriting in weekly letters to me. She filled me in on what my sisters were doing, where she and Barney planned to holiday, and asked after the children, but Rebecca was never mentioned. Nor was her name raised in the occasional telephone calls to which I treated myself when Ken was not around to cut me off after I had talked for five minutes. He did, however, scrutinise the monthly phone bill to check that I had not overstepped the limit he had imposed of one five-minute call a week. As he was no longer talking to any of his siblings, his use of the telephone was minimal.

After our first year in Sydney, Jan became a regular visitor for a while, usually when she was between work or men or both. The first I would know that she was gracing us with her presence was the sound of the children's squeals of 'Auntie Jannie's here' as they ran down the front steps to the taxi that had pulled up in the drive. Looking very Isadora Duncan as she swished a scarf over her shoulders, she hugged the children while the taxi driver unloaded wine, boxes of gourmet food and toys on to the front lawn. For the next few days she would fill our house with laughter, cigarette smoke and endless glasses of wine as she talked about her love life, the computer consultancy company she had recently left and the new one she was about to join. Eventually her knowledge of computers would take her to Western Australia, where she would start her own consultancy geared towards the mining industry.

Rebecca was never mentioned and it was not until I saw Jan's signature as next of kin on an application form Rebecca had completed in September 1973, requesting admission to the gender dysphoria program at the Parkville Psychiatric Clinic, that I realised that they had maintained some contact with each other despite Margie's edict.

Jan's interest in assisting Rebecca change gender appears to have been short-lived. Her name is not on any other copies of forms, notes or letters the Department of Health and Human services sent me in 2020. They did, however, provide me with a great deal of information about the issues with which Rebecca had been dealing, unbeknown to her family, for most of her life. As well as her application for admission to the clinic, she competed a General Information Questionnaire which was designed to provide the type of background information the psychiatrists needed to gauge the level of dysphoria in the applicants to the programme. On it, Rebecca claimed to have recently been working as a civil engineer for the firm of John Connell & Associates, the principal contractors engaged on the construction of the Melbourne Underground Rail Loop, but she gave no information about the capacity in which she was employed or how long she had worked there. She was unemployed at the time of completing the questionnaire.

There were also questions she had to answer about the extent of her cross-dressing – how long it had been going on and how frequently she dressed as a woman. To that she answered: 'I live as the opposite sex when I do not have to attend a male job'. In response to a further question about her choice of employment she wrote that the civil engineering job 'was the quickest to obtain and better paying than a female job'. She indicated that she was dissatisfied with the work she had during this period. She gave her address on the questionnaire as an apartment in Hawksburn Rd, South Yarra, which would have been within walking distance from Jan's apartment in Grange Road, Toorak. Although I could find no specific references to Hawksburn Road at the time Rebecca claimed to have lived there, from current real estate images the district would appear to remain largely untouched by the developers, with the streets lined with substantial homes. It is possible that the address in Hawksburn Rd was being used as a rooming house in the 1970s, but there is no evidence that there had been any formal subdivision on that site.

I also discovered from the questionnaire that Rebecca was not the only name she had experimented with as she was building up courage to committing herself to permanently changing her identity. She had also been known as Rebecca Wilson and Ruth Norton. To the questions relating to her marital status she stated that she had never been married nor had any children, although in the handwritten notes of interviews with Professor Ball she did admit to having been accused of getting a girl pregnant while working at Mount Isa.

Rebecca submitted the application form and questionnaire in September 1973 and had her first appointment with Professor Richard Ball at the Parkville Psychiatric Clinic at the end of October 1973.

Copies of Ball's copious notes of all their meetings over the following decade were included in the material I received from DHHS. Many were handwritten in atrocious handwriting and took hours to decipher, but they provided an insight into the secret world which Rebecca had been forced to inhabit since childhood because there was nobody in her family, school or community in whom she could confide.

Ball's notes also allowed me to appreciate the warmth and humanity of this man who, with a handful of medical professionals in Australia and elsewhere accepted that gender dysphoria was a serious medical condition rather than the whim of disillusioned individuals, and that it needed to be treated as such.

The first to reach this understanding in Melbourne and to treat patients accordingly was Dr Herbert Bower, who began to see people with different gender identities from 1951, using knowledge he had gleaned from publications surrounding high profile cases that had been sensationalised in the media, such as the tragic death of Lili Elbe, the first person to undergo transition surgery in 1930, and the American GI who became Christine Jorgensen following a penectomy in Denmark in 1952 and became a world-wide celebrity. She returned to the United States to have a vaginoplasty under the supervision of Dr Harry Benjamin, who would later join a pioneering group of doctors at Johns Hopkins Hospital in Baltimore in quietly opening the first sex reassignment surgery clinic in America. It was Benjamin who was responsible for differentiating between transsexualism and transvestism.

While their work encouraged worldwide interest in gender dysphoria, the clinic at Johns Hopkins came under attack from the more conservative elements of the hospital staff and the public and was closed down. Other clinics offering transgender surgery opened quietly in Europe and in exotic places like Casablanca, under the French gynaecologist Georges Burou. In Melbourne, the foundation of the Cato Chair of Psychiatry at Melbourne University in 1963 and the arrival from the United Kingdom of Richard Ball, who already had experience working in the gender dysphoria field, led to the establishment of an academic unit attached to the Mental Health Research Unit in Parkville. Despite experiencing considerable resistance to studying this aspect of human behaviour, he persisted with his research for his doctoral thesis, which focused on confused sexual identity, plasticity of gender roles in children and variation of sexual attraction in adults.

Largely as a result of his work, the Victorian Health Department established a Transexualism Consultative Clinic in Parkville in 1969 and the first surgeries were performed subsequently by Dr Hunter Fry at Royal Melbourne Hospital. The questionnaire which Rebecca completed was devised at about the same time. It gave Ball a starting point to begin his interviews with his clients.

According to Ball's notes, Rebecca was having great difficulty getting a job with which to support herself. The work with the civil engineering company she had mentioned on the questionnaire had dried up after only a few months and she could not return to her chosen field of mining engineering because too many people knew about the Mount Isa Rodeo dinner incident. She told Ball that she would only go for job interviews in the future dressed as a woman, and although she had been for two in the time since applying to join the program, one as a restaurant kitchen hand and another at a store cosmetic counter, she was unsuccessful and was living on money she had in the bank, which she said was $500.

The details Rebecca provided about her family and upbringing led Ball to describe Margie in his notes as an authoritarian figure. She appeared to him as a domineering person who tolerated no argument from her children, and they in turn discovered early in life that it was easier to let her dominate than to have a confrontation with her. Rebecca admitted that there were no strong bonds between herself and her father, who had little authority in the home. Of her four sisters, she only had a good rapport with Jan, the middle child of the family. She did not have much to do with the two youngest sisters and although she didn't name me, it was obvious that I was the sister with whom she didn't get on because there was strong competition between us and we argued.

Surprisingly, Ball did not ask about her education under the Christian Brothers in Ballarat. While the hierarchy of the church and the religious orders were still managing to hide the practice of paedophilia in schools and parishes from the public during the early 1970s, it would be surprising if Ball did not know of its existence or question whether his patients had been subjected to interference by priests or brothers with whom they had been in contact. Two decades later, Ball would have to come face to face with the extent of paedophilia in the Catholic Church when he came out of retirement to act as an independent medical professional for Carelink, a part of the Melbourne Response into child abuse by priests of the Melbourne Archdiocese, interviewing victims and arranging for them to receive treatment from a variety of providers including psychologists and psychiatrists. During this time, he met regularly with Archbishop George Pell.

In 1973 though, Ball was interested in Rebecca's lack of sexual education and experience. He asked her about her friendships in the past and at the time of the interview. She told him that she had no friends, although she had been to a few transvestite parties. Mostly she spent her leisure time reading, listening to light opera and musical comedy and doing yoga. She said that she had been receiving hormone injections since June 1973, so Ball sent her for a medical examination and for chromosome tests which came back as expected Normal male Karytype 46 XY. He also sought her permission to contact the Brisbane doctor who had treated her for drug addiction.

By the time Ball saw her again on 28 December 1973, two days before her 33rd birthday, she had changed her address to a unit in Toorak Road. Initially she would not tell him who she was living with, but eventually admitted that she had taken a job as a live-in housekeeper for a wealthy elderly man who she said was single. She was disgusted with the situation in which she found herself and was not happy with the regulations he imposed on her, but she could get no other work. He paid her only $10 a week on top of her keep. She indicated that he was gay and wanted a relationship with her.

Over the next 18 months Rebecca met regularly with the Professor and each time the questions he asked centred around her adjustment to living as a female. While he was satisfied with her progress in that regard, he was less than happy with her ongoing living arrangements. Comments like 'still with the old boy' could be found in the report of each meeting. Each time she told him that she was fed up with the arrangement and wanted to find a job that paid more money, but was having no success. At the end of May 1974, she must have thought she had a new job lined up because Ball wrote that she was looking for a flat and that her departure from the 'old boy' was imminent, even though he was rather distressed at the thought of losing her. The job obviously did not eventuate, as she was still with the 'old boy' in July and prospects did not seem bright.

The Captain

After we had adjusted to the shock of the relocation to New South Wales, we began making the long journey down the Hume Highway to visit Margie and Barney and to attend the weddings of Liz and Louise. Once Emma and Geoffrey were at school, I was making an annual pilgrimage to Melbourne with them and Phillip in my little car, until Ken fell out with the directors of the chemical company he moved to after he left Unilever, and I was forced to take over financial responsibility for the family while he waited for them to see how invaluable he had been and invite him back to the company on his terms. They never did.

It was on one of the school holiday trips in the late 1970s that Margie told me she had been visited by Rebecca, although to her she was still 'Rob' and 'he'. Rebecca had hired a car and driven out to Box Hill to collect her academic certificates and other work-related papers she intended to have reissued in her new name so she could begin applying for suitable employment.

Noting my very homemade appearance, Margie waxed lyrical about the clothes Rebecca was wearing – a finely pleated skirt, a silk blouse and a beautiful fitted jacket, all of which she told me had been bought at Melbourne's upmarket fashion store George's in Collins Street. Rebecca's hair, lightened to a honey blonde colour and worn in a page boy style fashionable at the time, was a vast improvement on my pony tail. They treated her to tea and cake while the documents she needed were found, but she gave them very little information about what she had been doing since 1973 except to tell Margie that she was sharing an apartment in Toorak with a retired military man she referred to only as 'The Captain'. While Margie was obviously pleased to see Rebecca again, that did not mean that there would be any relaxation of her edict that we refrain from talking about her to anyone outside the family.

Almost a decade later, when I had sold the picture framing business I had started to keep the family afloat and left Ken, I was once again able to take the drive down to Melbourne, this time with only Phillip for company, as Emma had joined the Air Force and was studying at the Australian Defence Force Academy in Canberra and Geoffrey was training and competing as a figure skater in Canada. We arrived in Box Hill to be told that we had been invited to join Margie and Barney for lunch with Rebecca and the Captain in Toorak.

At fifteen years of age, Phillip was very nervous about meeting someone about whom he knew very little, but once he found that Rebecca was serving for lunch a whole salmon she had bought at Prahran Market that morning, he relaxed. While he told her all about the fish he had caught, I took a seat in the dining room and listened to Margie prattling on to a wizened old man in a wheelchair, which had been parked at the top of the dining room table beneath a portrait of a man in full military uniform. He seemed not to know who we were or what we were doing at his table. Once the fish and vegetables were brought to the table for us to help ourselves, Rebecca sat beside the old man spooning into him a mashed-up version of our meal while keeping up chatter on all manner of topics, none of which I remember. Barney, Phillip and I were keen to leave as soon as we could afterwards.

I never saw the old man again, nor did I give him much thought before I began working on Rebecca's biography. As she only rarely mentioned him during the conversations we had in later years, the only clue to his identity, apart from the fact that he must have served in the Australian Army to earn the title of Captain, was that she sometimes referred to him as Ferdie. From the way she talked about the apartment in Toorak Road, I got the impression that he had lived there for some time before they met so, on the off chance that he had owned it, I began to search its history at the Land Titles Office in Melbourne. Starting with the present owner, I could establish who the immediately previous owner was and so on, until I arrived at 1989 to find that the unit was part of the deceased estate of Ferdinand Adrian Nelken, who had died in September that year leaving everything he owned to Rebecca Michelle Norton. With his full name and date of birth I was able to develop a profile for this man who had played an important part in Rebecca's life for quite a long time. The Captain was born in 1897 in Woollahra in New South Wales to Leo and Eva Nelken, who had married two years earlier at the Great Synagogue in Sydney. While Leo was Jewish, describing himself as either an Austrian or Polish

Russian Jew, depending on the circumstances in which he had to provide proof of his identity, Eva was probably Irish or of Irish descent, having the maiden surname of Moody on their Register of Marriage and having come from Bendigo.

Leo Nelken was described variously as an insurance salesman or an employee of the Taxation Department in the frequent mentions of his interactions with the police in both New South Wales and Victoria, usually for being engaged in drunken brawls due to his propensity to assume that he was being racially abused. He provided poorly for his wife and two sons who left him to return to Victoria, where she opened a rooming house in St Kilda, but he was a frequent visitor there and continued to be violent to her when drunk, on one occasion chasing her through the boarding house with an axe.

His reputation as a German spy, gained during a dispute in a hotel in which he was drinking, threatened to prevent his son's determination to enlist in 1916, with the matter ending in court. Nelken senior was, however, able to demonstrate to the magistrate that he was neither German nor a spy, claiming to have lived in Australia for about forty-six years and to be a naturalised Australian, but could not provide papers. It is possible that he had New Zealand citizenship. Nevertheless, the recruiting officer was satisfied that the recruit Nelken posed no threat to the country or the war effort.

Ferdinand Adrian Nelken was eighteen-and-a-half when he applied to enlist according to the files which are freely available to be downloaded from the National Archives of Australia World War I collection. He gave his occupation as travelling salesman for the Sydney firm of Simonson Pty Ltd, but he had returned to Victoria to enlist, giving his father's address of Collins House, Collins Street, as his temporary abode. He was five foot, three and a half inches tall (161 cm). After initial training he was sent overseas with the 7th Battalion, leaving Melbourne on the 11th September 1916. By December he was fighting in France, where he was wounded in October 1917.

Initial reports via the Red Cross indicated that the injury was to a shoulder, which prompted Leo Nelken to write to the Officer in Charge of Base Records demanding clarification. He was told that Ferdinand had received a gunshot wound to the leg, causing a fracture. He had been admitted to hospital in Birmingham on 4th November 1917 with a fractured right thigh and was transferred to the Australian Auxiliary hospital on 16th January 1918, before being returned to Australia on the *Kenilworth Castle* for recovery, but he was clearly not finished with the Army. On the 22nd of March 1919 he requested leave to be discharged from his current battalion so that he could transfer to the Pay Corps. He was granted his request and promoted to Corporal.

Although all the records from World War II are also housed by the National Archives, they are not available until a request is made and a fee paid for them to be digitised. In the file I received I found that Nelken had continued his attachment to the AIF during the interwar period on a part-time basis, engaging in training programmes, where available, so that by the time war broke out again in 1939, he was re-enlisted as an Acting Lieutenant, at the age of forty-two years and eight months but there was little information provided about postings and his duties except that he was promoted to Acting Captain in 1940. And when his appointment was terminated in March 1942, he offered his services in an honorary capacity, provided that he could continue wearing his uniform.

Around the time I was searching for information about The Captain, I was contacted by Professor Noah Riseman who had been told about the biography I was writing by a mutual colleague. At the time he was compiling a Report for the Australian Professional Association for Trans Health, A History of Trans Health, I agreed to share with him the material I had concerning Rebecca's experience with the Parkville Psychiatric Centre. As he had access to material in the National Archives which has not been digitised, he offered to search for information about the Captain's World War II military record for which I was most grateful.

It seems Nelkin was offered administrative duties at the Munitions works in Footscray and at Deer Park, using his own car to travel between the two sites. He continued to use his own car, for which he received petrol vouchers, once he was transferred to Area Command to assist in monitoring compassionate leave applications. In August 1944 his employment was questioned by senior military personnel, one of whom accused Nelken in an expletive-laden attack of using his petrol ration to further his own import/export business. This sparked a three-month long dispute, reaching the attention of the Commander in Chief of the Army who demanded resolution of the matter.

Nelken got satisfaction, but his association with the army was over.

However, he did continue to strut around in his uniform and continued to be known to friends and associates as The Captain. In 1947 he had the portrait, which I had seen on the dining room wall of the Toorak Road apartment, painted by the artist Rashid Bey, who was making quite a name for himself in Toorak society in the years after WWII.

Surgery

It was The Captain's name that I found in the space reserved for next of kin on the copy of the admissions form for the Royal Melbourne Hospital 20th June 1975. But as I read through the records that accompanied the admissions form, I became aware that The Captain's presence in Rebecca's life was not without controversy. Professor Ball was not impressed that she had taken a live-in job as a domestic servant for The Captain, who paid her a pittance, and seemed unable to move on, even though it was clear that Ball saw the arrangement as a barrier to her successful gender affirmation. It was not until she was able to tell Professor Ball during her second year in the gender programme that, while she intended to continue to live with The Captain, she had found work as a machinist at a factory called Universal Textiles in Prahran, that he was prepared to view her as a likely candidate for gender affirmation.

On that basis he arranged for her to meet with the panel of surgeons, psychiatrists and other medical professionals he had assembled, so they could question her understanding of the process she wanted to undertake and assess the likelihood of it being successful. They were clearly impressed with her ability to answer their questions and requested a second meeting in late May 1975.

At that meeting Rebecca was just as impressive. They noted that she was well-groomed and conservatively dressed as a woman and was able to answer all the questions asked of her. It was obvious that she understood the process she was committed to undergo and was looking forward to living as a woman. There is no indication in the transcripts of either of these meetings that they asked her for proof that she was in fact working at the textile factory.

While the date of the surgery was set for the last Sunday in June 1975, there was another step she had to take before she could proceed. She had to take the legal document she had been sent to a solicitor, so it could be read in his presence. He was then required to confirm to Ball and the Medical Registrar of Royal Melbourne Hospital that she understood the legal ramifications of the procedure. From the copy I received in 2020, it was obvious that it had been designed to protect the medical profession from litigation should the surgery fail to meet her expectations, or if she regretted having committed to an irrevocable procedure. Particular attention was drawn to the clause in the document which stated that the surgery would not produce a fully functional organ, and that it would be necessary for her to receive post-operative psychiatric treatment and future surgery, as the initial operation was only the first in a staged process.

She took the document to a solicitor and barrister in Prahran called Diamond, who read and explained it to her and provided a letter addressed to Professor Ball assuring him that she fully understood 'the nature and quality of the matters so explained'.

On 20th June 1975 Rebecca brought the form with her to the Royal Melbourne Hospital, where she was under strict instructions not to present to the Admissions Office, but to go directly to Ward 1 North, where she would be met by a Dr Hurley, who would witness her signature on the legal document and satisfy himself that she understood all its provisions. She would then undergo admission formalities, including the admissions form mentioned earlier, with The Captain nominated as next of kin. He had apparently accompanied her to the hospital, contrary to the expectations of the staff. The fact that the patients were admitted to a part of the hospital which was some distance from the main Admissions Office so that they were unlikely to face the disapproving glares of those who thought that these gender altering procedures were immoral, added to the clandestine nature of the whole procedure. They certainly had made no provision for friends and family to wait while the surgery was performed. Nevertheless, the Captain remained at the hospital, obviously close enough to be by her side as soon as she was wheeled out of surgery into the waiting ambulance which carried her back to the Parkville Psychiatric Unit, where she would spend the next week or so in recovery.

According to the patient notes which were filled in by the charge nurses on duty, the Captain was a frequent and generally unwelcome presence during much of Rebecca's stay at the Psychiatric Unit. He was, however, the only comfort she had as she recovered from the surgery which involved the removal of both her testicles and her penis and the fashioning of the skin in which they had been encased into a vagina and labia. Hopefully he was there when she received the bad news that the surgeons had been unable to find enough skin to fashion a satisfactory vagina. It was going to be too short and narrow for her to have meaningful intercourse. She would require additional surgery, but there was no guarantee that the problem could be rectified. There was also a risk that other organs such as her urethra would sustain further damage and would require repair. The scar tissue which developed during this and subsequent operations also created more problems, which remained with her for the rest of her life.

Rebecca was obviously disappointed with the shortcomings of her surgery, but not with her decision to submit herself to it, as she told Professor Ball on several occasions. As she had entered the surgical programme as an outpatient of the Royal Melbourne Hospital, he sent her there to see the operating surgeon, Hunter Fry, where she found herself joining the queue of patients waiting on a first come, first seen basis, often waiting for several hours. She pleaded with Ball to refer her to Fry's private rooms, so she could make an appointment and see him in a timely manner, but Ball would not be moved. As she had entered the system as a public patient she would have to remain so, and wait her turn to see the doctors at the hospital.

After several letters complaining about the unfairness of this decision, particularly because it hampered her ability to seek employment in her chosen profession, Ball gave in and agreed to discuss her situation with Fry, but it was not until October 1981 that Fry wrote to Dr Grigor, the Chief

Clinical Officer at the Parkville Psychiatric Unit about taking Rebecca out of the transsexual programme so that he could treat her privately and another six months before she was able to get an appointment to see him. He arranged to admit her to the Epworth Plastic Surgery Unit on 25th May 1982, so he could do an examination under anaesthetic. He offered her some options, including incising the vagina and inserting a graft taken from her groin. This operation was performed at Epworth on 13th July 1982. Nine days later, Fry reported to Grigor that he had been able to extend the length and diameter of the vagina, but a fistula had developed and was a cause for some concern. It would need repair, which could in turn damage the bladder. He was calling in a urologist for advice.

Clearly dissatisfied with the situation, in October 1983 Rebecca applied to the Health Department and the Mental Health Authority for access to the documents relating to her treatment in the Parkville Psychiatric Unit. After much deliberation over whether the documents could be released, Dr Grigor met with Rebecca on 8th December 1983 so that she could read them in his presence. He gave his explanation for her request:

> the reason behind the request ...was to look further into the rather unsatisfactory circumstances concerning the surgical outcome to her transsexual operation. Despite all due care being exercised, the vaginal reconstruction was not of sufficient length to be satisfactory to either the surgeon or the patient, and further reconstruction surgery has proceeded over the years. A vasico-vaginal fistula resulted from the earlier surgery and has again recurred,

and the patient will be once more consulting her plastic surgeon, Mr Hunter Fry, and it is likely that she will require further surgery to the exterior wall of the vaginal reconstruction in order to repair this fistula between her bladder and vagina. It may be that this very sensible and competent person may require some further modest assistance in identifying people to provide second opinions. This will be in the surgical rather than in the psychiatric area.

Another plastic surgeon was found for her in Simon Ceber, who had probably assisted Hunter Fry at the operation performed at Epworth in 1982. Ceber operated two more times, in 1984 and 1988 at the Queen Victoria Hospital, to remake her vagina and to repair damage to her urethra and the fistula which had developed as a result of earlier operations. He did not see her again after 1988.

Getting the Paperwork in Order

Amongst the correspondence which flowed between Rebecca and Professor Ball in the years after the surgery were a couple of letters which indicated that, despite her disappointment with the surgery, she had no regrets about her decision to change gender. She was even making plans to make herself employable in the mining industry once again. By October 1977 she had managed to get some work using her civil engineering qualifications, possibly in the construction industry, as there were several large projects underway in Melbourne at the time. But it was night shift, so she could not present herself at Ball's rooms in Parkville to get a script for the hormone Estigyn. She wrote him a long letter asking him to send it to the Toorak Road address she was still sharing with The Captain.

She also told him that she was in the process of getting her academic qualifications and employment certificates reissued in her new name and that there was some urgency in this as she had details of a great job in the Northern Territory for which she intended to apply. In the meantime, she had enrolled in a computer course at RMIT, which at this time was a college of advanced education, in an effort to improve her employment prospects.

The precious Queensland Department of Mines Mine Manager's ticket had been Rebecca's first concern, and probably necessary for her to be considered for the position in the Northern Territory, though there is no evidence that she actually sent off an application for it. She did, however, write to the Secretary of Mines at the Queensland Department of Mines on July 17 1977, explaining that she had changed her name by deed poll following her sex change.

> … I enquire whether or not I may apply to have that certificate re-issued to my present name and what documents and fees are required.
>
> Further, could you advise me of the price of the current *Mines Act, Regulations for Metalliferous Mines, Amendments* and any other publications relating to practising as a mine manager in Queensland. I am informed that your department has stated no objection to the employment of females in mines. Could you please confirm …

This was of course an issue she had never before had to consider, but it was now of vital importance. Although a ruling by the Conciliation and Arbitration Commission in 1973 had finally granted an equal minimum wage to all Australians, regardless of their sex, it was still very much a man's world and distinctions were made between what could be considered male and female work, with that done mostly by women attracting lower wages. Well into the 1980s companies could and did declare certain roles within their organisations as male-only jobs, so that even if a woman had the right qualifications, she could be refused employment. Women were also denied advancement in most companies, with all managerial positions held by men. Banks routinely denied loans to women, as I found to my cost in 1985 when I wanted to borrow money to upgrade a piece of equipment for the picture framing business I was running successfully. I could only get the money I needed if I had the written permission of Ken Blee from whom, by this time, I was estranged.

Fortunately for Rebecca, the Secretary of the Board of Examiners for the Queensland Department of Mines wrote to her by return mail asking that she provide documentation of her change of name along with the original Mine Manager's certificate. He also advised her as to where she could obtain copies of the *Mining Act 1968-1976* and the *Mines Regulation Act 1964 –1968*. Regarding employment of females in mines, he quoted Section 46 of the *Mines Regulations Act* which said that, 'No female shall be employed underground in a mine except with the approval of the Chief Inspector'.

Undeterred by this information, Rebecca forwarded her deed poll certificate along with a rather worn and tattered Mine Manager's ticket with an explanation that it had been displayed on all sites which she had managed, and at times it had been subject to harsh weather conditions. The Board of Examiners of the Queensland Mines Department met on August 5 and approved the re-issuing of the Mine Manager's certificate in Rebecca's name and she was informed on 10 August. She received it together with a letter of acknowledgement that she was required to sign in the presence of a witness. The Captain acted as her witness.

At about the same time, Rebecca approached the Women's Co-ordinator of the Victorian Mines Department about the possibility of applying for a Victorian Mine Manager's Ticket. In her letter to Professor Ball in October 1977 she told him that she had written to the Minister for Mines but had not received a reply. She was eventually able to satisfy the Board of Examiners of the Department of Minerals and Energy who, on the 13th August 1980, issued her with a Certificate of Competency in the areas of Gold and Minerals.

Although I was unable to find any record of her letter to Melbourne University asking that her academic record be reissued in her new name, her request seems to have received prompt attention as the copy I found in her certificate file was dated October 1977. She received a less positive response to her request that the certificates of her two diplomas from the School of Mines, Ballarat, be reissued. The School had amalgamated with the Ballarat Teachers' College to become the Ballarat School of Advanced Education and I was told that its Registrar could not in conscience countenance the concept of gender change. After several follow-up requests, he did accept that his stance could hamper Rebecca's work opportunities, so the certificates were eventually reissued in her new name.

Rebecca also wrote to the two men who had endorsed her original application for membership of the Institute of Engineers, one of whom was a Deputy Vice Chancellor of Townsville University and the other a Professor of Engineering of Melbourne University. Their paths had apparently crossed during her Mount Isa days, and both were happy enough to accept her request that the Institute of Engineers re-issue the Certificate of Membership in her new name.

She didn't wait for her old boss from Mount Isa, who was overseas at the time, to endorse the re-issue of her Membership Certificate of the Australasian Institute of Mining and Metallurgy. Instead she took herself into the offices of the AusIMM in Lygon St, Carlton and explained to the two secretaries who ran the office that she wanted to renew the membership she had held in the name of Robert Michael Norton since her first year at Melbourne University, when she had become a Student Member. That membership had been upgraded to a Graduate Member in 1964 after she had been working at Mount Isa for nine months. In 1968 she had become a full Member, but with everything going on in her life she had let her membership lapse.

As the notion of anyone changing gender was still quite alien in 1977, Rebecca's appearance and her request must have shocked the two secretaries, but they appear to have handled the situation with ease, taking her particulars and explaining that the decision to reinstate the membership under a new name would be a matter for the Board. That too appears to have received no opposition from the Directors, who agreed to reinstate her full membership.

The one certificate she could not change immediately was her birth certificate. As Professor Noah Riseman has pointed out in his book *Transgender Australia: A History Since 1910*, published by Melbourne University Press in 2023, politicians in both the Federal and State jurisdictions were slow to act on requests that birth certificates and passports be able to recognise the current gender of applicants rather than their gender at birth. As the issuing of birth certificates was a matter for the States, the Federal government left the decisions relating to requests by transgender applicants for the re-issuing of certificates up to State jurisdictions.

While in the late 1970s the government was prepared to allow passports to be issued in which there was no requirement on the part of applicants to have their gender noted, from 1980 this became much harder, as proof of gender became mandatory on all applications, and from 1983, applications had to be made in person rather than posted, as had previously been acceptable. After much lobbying by the transgender community, the rules were changed the following year to allow people who had medical proof of having undergone transgender surgery to obtain a passport which acknowledged their chosen gender.

Unfortunately, the passport could not be used to obtain any other identity documents in their chosen gender. It was up to activists in each State to lobby State Attorneys to change the law. They were slow to act, with Rebecca only receiving her Certificate of Birth Registration on 23rd November 1989. While all other details on it were correct and she was listed as female, her birth date was incorrect. It was listed as 30th November 1940. She was born on 30 December 1940. There is no indication that she asked for it to be reissued correctly.

Working for the Big Australian

In late 1980, Rebecca rang to invite me to join her and her boyfriend for drinks at one of the swish hotels down by the Rocks in Sydney – a surprise to say the least. I presume she had been given my number by Margie, indicating that while we were still under the embargo she had imposed on us, she and Rebecca were in regular contact. Out of curiosity as much as anything else, I accepted the invitation, leaving the children in the not very capable hands of their father, and drove into the city, something I did rarely at the time. On the way in I was concerned that I wouldn't recognise her and that we would have nothing in common to talk about, but I needn't have worried. She spotted me as soon as I walked through the big glass door entrance of the hotel and came to greet me.

She was wearing a light-coloured floral dress, belted at the waist over a flared skirt which swished as she came down the steps from the lounge bar to greet me. Her face was familiar despite the expertly applied make up. Her hair was as Margie had described it two years earlier, deep blonde and sculptured into a page boy style. She was wearing stiletto-heeled shoes which meant that she had to bend down to kiss me on the cheek. She introduced me to the very handsome Richard, the boyfriend, who smiled but otherwise didn't open his mouth except to sip the champagne she ordered for the three of us. I expect he was used to listening, not talking, as he would have had as much difficulty getting a word in as I did during the brief time we were together.

I can't remember her asking after my husband or the children, or what life was like for us in Sydney. Nor did she give me any opportunity to tell her about the Bachelor of Arts degree I had embarked on at Macquarie University. Given the opinion she often expressed during conversations we had in her later years, she would probably have rebuked me for abandoning my scientific training for the Arts, which she considered a waste of time and energy. On this occasion though, the conversation was entirely about her and her importance to BHP, the Big Australian, which she had apparently been invited to join because of her vast and varied experience in the mining of non-ferrous metals across the continent. It would appear that this work was regularly taking her to Western Australia, where I suspect she had met and formed a relationship with the silent Richard, but whether he also worked for BHP or was part of the furniture of the mines she visited, I did not find out. After three glasses of champagne I was getting anxious about the drive home to Winston Hills, so I said my goodbyes and left. It would be some years before I saw her again. By then the silent Richard was no longer in her life and she had moved on from BHP.

Though I can to this day remember the dress, the stiletto heels and the long cigarette holder on which she puffed occasionally while she talked, when I went to write about this period of Rebecca's life, I could remember very little of what she had told me about her work for BHP, nor initially could I find out. All attempts to reach anyone in BHP who could confirm Rebecca's connection with the company and the role she had played during the years she said she was employed there went nowhere. If the company employed an archivist, that person was inaccessible to the public. I had the same lack of success in trying to contact the Human Resources Department of the company.

I did, however, have one possible source of information. My daughter Emma remembered that just after she left the Air Force in 1996 she was invited to a birthday party for Rebecca at the home of a friend of hers in East Melbourne, where she met a man called Hugh Mackinnon, home for a short visit from his work in mining in Kazakhstan. He told her that he had worked alongside Rebecca at BHP but gave no details. I was aware in later years that she had maintained occasional contact by email with a man working in Kazakhstan and that on a trip back to Melbourne he had visited her. As I felt sure that she would not have had many acquaintances living and working in Central Asia, I went in search of an email address for a man called Hugh among the few possessions I gathered up from her apartment after helping her move into care in 2012. Not expecting a swift response, I sent off an email to the address I found and was surprised to receive a prompt reply. He had retired from mining and was living in Melbourne with his family. He had heard about Rebecca's passing and offered to come to Ballarat to tell me all he knew about her time with BHP.

They had both been members of the Resource Technology Minerals Division of BHP, a small group of engineers and geologists tasked with seeking out and evaluating new and existing mining prospects for the expanding company. When he joined the division in 1979, Rebecca had already been there for about a year. He knew nothing of her background and nor, he thought, did any of the team, although no-one seems to have questioned how she came to be working for the company, given its policy at the time of not employing women in mining and associated roles. Later I discovered that gender rules could be broken to satisfy a need, in this case expertise in deep lead mining that BHP was keen to embark upon having, up to this time, been predominantly engaged in open cut iron and coal mining. Rebecca's Mount Isa experience alone was enough to earn an invitation to join the Division.

Hugh told me he found her fascinating, as did the other men in the Division. She presented as a very confident woman, who held the floor whenever the team were all in the office, which was rare, as their investigations took them to mine sites all over the country. He acknowledged her enormous talent, her brilliant mind and photographic memory, but he admitted that she would assail anyone who would listen to her. Her fault was that she never knew when to shut up, and after a time her audience simply zoned out. Surprisingly though, it seems that none of the team suspected that Rebecca had not always been a woman, despite her most consistent fashion accessory being a chiffon scarf worn around her neck. In the office she was always magnificently dressed, courtesy of

George's, the most expensive department store in Melbourne, which was a stone's throw from the BHP Head Office in Collins Street. She always wore dresses, stockings and high heeled shoes when she was in the office, but never trousers, even though the pant suit had been growing in popularity during the 1970s. They didn't find out about her change of gender until one of the engineers visited Mount Isa bearing greetings from her to a colleague she had worked alongside in the 1960s. He asked how *Bob* was settling into her new life in Melbourne.

Although they never worked on the same projects, Hugh was able to tell me that one of Rebecca's first assignments with the Resource Technology Minerals Division involved a recently discovered lead/zinc deposit at a place called Blendevale in the Kimberley region of Western Australia, about fifteen to twenty kilometres south-east of Fitzroy Crossing, and that there had been some consternation from senior management about her being sent there because there were no facilities on the site suitable for a woman. There was only a roughly constructed mining camp which was shared by male staff and miners alike, with the nearest decent accommodation at Derby, 300km away. But having seen pictures of the mine camp at Hatches Creek where she had lived while she managed that mine in the late 1960s, I expect she would have been undaunted by the conditions of the camp at Blendevale, even if the men she had to work with were uncomfortable about sharing them with a woman.

Rebecca had been commissioned by BHP to assess the technical and financial prospects of developing the project from tests being carried out under her supervision. It had already been determined that the ore was similar to that which is found in other lead-zinc deposits throughout the world, but most particularly in North America, where the ore is called Mississippi Valley-Type. This necessitated a fact-finding mission to the United States, most probably to the St. Joseph Lead Company in Missouri, where the zinc/lead composite was successfully being mined and treated.

While Hugh could tell me very little about who accompanied Rebecca to the United States, he was able to give me the names of a couple of men who had worked for BHP at the same time. They in turn passed me on to other mining engineers, some of whom knew Rebecca, and others who had heard tales about her. Thus began another grapevine of old miners, but the information I acquired from them was very patchy. Several of my informants knew Rebecca had gone to America to study the zinc mining, and that she was accompanied by two geologists, but nobody could tell me their names or how I could contact them.

My interest, of course, was not what she had learned about zinc mining but how she was received by the management of the mines she visited and the men she travelled with and met along the way. In her later years she talked about America, particularly the Midwest, as if she had spent many months studying the population as well as the zinc, but I am left to wonder what impression she made on the people with whom she worked in the mines she visited, and whether any of them were experienced enough in the ways of the world to suspect that she had not always been a woman.

I continued to contact members of the old miners' grapevine until I found someone who had worked alongside her on the Blendevale project for a short while. From him I discovered that the results of tests on the ore body had not lived up to expectations and that it was decided that more exploration would be needed before any decisions could be made about the likelihood of BHP investment in the establishment of a mine on the site. He took over the project, while Rebecca moved on to the assessment of an old gold mine called Nevoria in the Southern Cross greenstone belt of Western Australia, 10km southeast of Marvel Loch, which BHP was considering purchasing and reopening.

The region had been heavily mined by individual prospectors since the beginning of the 20th century, with ownership of the Nevoria Lease passing through several hands until the 1960s, when Western Mining Corporation briefly opened a mine there. Rebecca's task was to supervise the de-watering of the mine to provide access down the old shaft and into the workings so that an assessment of the potential gold yield could be ascertained. The process, which took the best part of twelve months, was to no avail and the results were disappointing. It was suspected that the samples provided by the prospective vendors had been falsified and the project was abandoned.

It seems that during these extended periods away from the Melbourne office she was always made welcome by the engineers and geologists of BHP's Minerals Exploration Division in Western Australia, even though she was well aware that some of those who had known her both before and after her gender affirmation took the opportunity to acquaint new graduates with the complexities of her life. One of the men who had worked in the Perth office during the time Rebecca was a frequent visitor was Cory Williams, who was happy to share the stories he could remember. He told me about a lunch he and another engineer had with Rebecca at a prominent hotel in Perth. They were escorted by the head waiter to one of the best tables in the dining room. As she sat down she commented that had she been dining on her own she would have been shown to a table on the back wall, probably screened off from the other diners by a palm tree in a pot. Cory wasn't sure whether the head waiter disapproved of women dining on their own or if he knew about Rebecca's gender affirmation.

Another story involved the education of a raw young graduate at the bottom of the Nevoria shaft on being introduced to Rebecca dressed in overalls, boots and hard hat with the chiffon scarf around her neck. When asked his opinion of her, he reckoned that she would probably be good in the front row of a rugby scrum. The geologist accompanying him told him, 'in geology, as in life, all is not as it seems'.

Perhaps this remark could have applied equally to the silent Richard with whom I drank champagne at Rebecca's expense in the Rocks in 1980. In 2020, when I was reading through the Parkville Psychiatric Centre correspondence, I came across a comment in a letter written in April 1982 to the surgeon who had performed Rebecca's surgery from one of the psychiatrists who had been intimately involved in her ongoing care. He was impressed by the way she 'had picked up her career and adjusted to her new lifestyle in her profession where she was known previously and is still known as a transexual by a number of her co-workers'. He went on to express his disappointment that the surgery had not produced the desired outcome from a technical point of view, as she had told him about a romantic attachment which had soured because of the inadequacies of the surgery. He wrote:

> ... she became emotionally attached to a person while on site and this relationship could not proceed very far; the partner suspected something and checked out with his friends and discovered that Rebecca was a transexual and this reawakened some interest in the matter, which Rebecca had to deal with ...

Mining Consultant

It seems that while Rebecca was more than happy to share her knowledge of mining with whoever would listen, she was much more tight-lipped about her private life. According to Hugh Mackinnon, the men of BHP's Resource Technology Minerals Division knew very little about her except that she had a gentleman friend with whom she shared an apartment in Toorak Rd, South Yarra and that they regularly attended race meetings at all three of Melbourne's race courses. That, her workmates assumed, accounted for the extensive wardrobe of dresses, shoes and handbags she paraded in the office.

They didn't know her friend's name or the toll her frequent trips to Western Australia was having on their relationship. I am sure that her frequent absences from Melbourne were a source of great concern for her, as they impacted on The Captain's wellbeing. He was, after all, about 80 years of age when she joined BHP and his health was deteriorating. While she could employ part-time housekeepers to cook and clean for him while she was in Western Australia, they were no substitute for the companionship she gave him.

She began making plans to leave BHP as early as

November 1982, when she purchased a shelf company in preparation for establishing herself as a mining consultant based in The Captain's living room in South Yarra. The company was called Twenty Seven Gozbarb Pty Ltd and had as its initial Directors the solicitor who supervised the purchase and his associate, along with herself and Jan, who gave Margie's and Barney's Box Hill address as her own. A month later, the registered address of the company was changed from the solicitor's office in Oakleigh to the address in Toorak Road, South Yarra. At the same time the solicitor and his associate resigned from the company, leaving Rebecca and Jan as the only Directors. By August of the following year, an application had been made to the National Companies and Securities Commission for the company name to be changed to Norton Mining Services Pty Ltd.

Jan was listed as a Director on all the documents relating to Norton Mining Services Pty Ltd which I was able to download, for a fee, from the National Companies and Securities Commission website, although it is unlikely that she had any input into Rebecca's business dealings, or that she signed any of the documents submitted under her name. Whoever was given the task of co-signing annual reports and statements of earnings was a very poor and inconsistent forger, but nobody in the Commission seemed to have noticed.

Jan's address remained that of the family home in Box Hill, although I doubt Margie and Barney were aware it had become the registered address of a Director of the company Rebecca had established. By the time it was operational, Jan was living and working in the computer industry in Chatswood in New South Wales and would move to Perth to start her own programming business targeted at the mining industry a few years later. That business would take her to mines all over Western Australia as well as to New Zealand, New Guinea and Indonesia until ill health forced her retirement. A sixty-a-day cigarette smoker for most of her adult life, she had developed such severe asthma by her early fifties that aeroplane travel was an impossibility. She had, in the meantime, met the pest exterminator Tom Bolvig on one of her visits to Christmas Island and they eventually married, moving to the Western Australian wheat belt town of Bruce Rock, where his services were in constant demand. By this time Rebecca's business was in sharp decline.

Initially Rebecca did all she could to promote her services, revitalising her memberships in professional organisations such as The Australasian Institute of Mining and Metallurgy and the Institute of Engineers. At the AusIMM she served on numerous committees and was Branch Secretary for a time, being rewarded for her efforts by being made a Fellow of the Institute. To achieve this award, according to the Proceedings published in the August 1987 AUSIMM bulletin, 'a member must have been engaged in *his* profession in mining, metallurgy, engineering or science for at least ten years during which period *he* shall have occupied a position of major responsibility for at least five years in the mining and/or metallurgical industries, or in government, educational or a research organisation concerned with those industries'. While there was no consideration for women being part of the mining industry, the Institute was obviously able to consider Rebecca's contribution to the industry both before and after her gender change. She was also awarded Fellowship status by the Institute of Engineers and was a member of the Victorian Chamber of Mines, from which she was granted a Mine Manager's Ticket to go with the one awarded by the Queensland Department of Mines.

In addition to being a Fellow of the AusIMM, she was invited to become a member of the Mineral Industry Consultants Association Inc. or MICA, as it was known. This organisation, established as a society within AusIMM in 1981, had as its members senior consultants who were experts in their respective fields within the mining industry. The objective of MICA was to function as an association of consultants providing technical advisory services to the mineral industry both within Australasia and worldwide. It also provided a common voice for its members to put forward their views on various issues which had a bearing on their specialised area of work in the consulting profession. In recognition of their involvement in MICA, members were invited to advertise their services in the bi-monthly bulletins of the Institute. Rebecca made full use of this opportunity.

Fellow members of MICA with whom I was able to talk had nothing but praise for her willingness to share her knowledge and expertise, but how successful she was at running her own business and attracting enough work to meet her financial needs is questionable. Judging from reports she lodged with the National Companies and Securities Commission, her business failed to register a profit in any year for which I was able to find records, and instead there was a growing debt which, by 1989, was in excess of $100,000. With no company books still in existence, it was impossible to know who her clients were and how much they contributed to the company's income. What seems certain was that their needs had to be met around the amount of time which was taken up firstly by Rebecca's philanthropic activities towards the mining industry and also by the increasing level of care The Captain required.

That was also difficult to ascertain until I received his medical records from the Department of Veterans Affairs with the help of Professor Noah Riseman, whose extensive work on the issues surrounding Aboriginal and LGBTQIA personnel in the Australian Armed Forces gave him access to archives which were out of reach to me at the time.

Because of The Captain's extensive record of service in both world wars, he was entitled to whatever treatment he needed through the Department of Veterans Affairs, including lengthy stays at the Heidelberg Repatriation Hospital and its rehabilitation service at Macleod Repatriation Hospital. The Department of Veterans Affairs could also arrange and pay for mobility aids and modifications to the bathroom and bedroom of the unit in Toorak Road so that The Captain could fend for himself for short periods when Rebecca was absent, but even these became of little use to him as his mobility deteriorated along with his self-confidence. He was relying on Rebecca to do everything for him, while at the same time being adamant that he would not contemplate moving into a nursing home.

He was hospitalised for nearly two months at the end

of 1984 so that he could undergo surgery for several problems associated with cancer in his prostate and for chronic renal failure. While the doctors were able to relieve some of his discomfort, he was in too fragile a state for any permanent improvements to be made. As it was, the recovery period was long, made longer by The Captain's refusal to cooperate with the staff caring for him. He insisted on being addressed by everyone who dealt with him as Captain, not Mr Nelken, and was very demanding of the staff. There were also signs of dementia. He was eventually discharged from the hospital in December 1984, with a walking frame to aid his mobility, but only after home visits by the district nurse and a physiotherapist had been arranged to assist Rebecca with his care.

Arrangements were made for The Captain to participate in a mobility group in the occupational therapy department of Heidelberg Hospital three mornings a week, with transport arranged by the Department of Veterans Affairs. While the benefits were negligible, Rebecca was able to attend to her clients, but by the middle of the next year there were more problems to contend with. The Captain's sight was failing and he was having difficulties with his teeth, requiring him to be spoon fed soft foods, which was how we found him when Phillip and I visited Rebecca with Margie and Barney in 1988.

The Captain's deterioration continued, according to the records kept by the Department of Veterans Affairs, so much so that the staff were concerned for Rebecca's wellbeing. By 1986 she was being deprived of sleep because The Captain could no longer distinguish night from day and was demanding her attention. The doctors prescribed stronger sedatives. Then Rebecca hurt her back lifting him and more respite care was arranged. This was to become a recurring event over the next few years, with the Department approving 14 days of respite care in a private hospital for The Captain every six weeks. As he was Jewish, a place was found for him at the Montefiore Home for the Aged in St Kilda Road.

While the medical and nursing staff were full of praise for the dedication Rebecca showed the old man, the administrative staff were not always so impressed. On the various forms they filled out over the ensuing five years they remained confused about the relationship between the old man and his carer. At times she was listed as Michelle Norton, the name The Captain preferred, and as his secretary, although on one form she was listed as his landlady. Occasionally *friend of his* was written beside her name but they baulked at referring to her as next of kin. They even went out of their way to find a real next of kin, which they succeeded in doing. Two elderly cousins were located in Malvern, but neither showed any interest in The Captain and did not visit him during any of his lengthy stays in hospital.

Mining in Pakistan

The demands of my picture-framing business, a disintegrating marriage and the needs of my three teenage children kept me from attending many of the extended family milestone celebrations during the 1980s, but at those for which I was able to travel to Melbourne, Margie made sure that any questions about Rebecca's absence would be dealt with in a manner that allowed no discussion. She had a number of stock explanations which she had decided we were all to use in the event an aunt or cousin asked, 'Where's Rob?' Her favourite, told with all the superiority her voice could muster was, 'Rob is working for the United Nations in Pakistan'.

I presume Rebecca had told Margie about a trip she had taken on behalf of the United Nations to Pakistan, because it would be hard to imagine that she would have conjured up such an excuse otherwise, but when I came to research this period of Rebecca's life the only mention in the curriculum vitae I had was in a list of assignments she had supposedly undertaken sometime in the 1980s. She did acknowledge that the sponsor of the trip was the United Nations and that it was to Kashmir, but she did not indicate when exactly this assignment took place, whether she participated as a member of a team, or whether she faced any difficulties as a woman in a country in which women, especially in the 1980s, had very few rights.

I do believe that the assignment in Kashmir or Pakistan must have taken place because, like the visit to the Midwest of the United States during her BHP days, the experience had made her an instant expert on the region generally. She would often regale me with her knowledge of the harsh weather conditions, the history of gem mining in the region, and the people and their politics, during those afternoons I spent in her little apartment in Ballarat sipping Irish whiskey while she drank cheap champagne, when all that was left of what could have been a brilliant career were the memories.

I never interrupted her as she talked or asked for details – I had adopted a policy of not questioning her on anything. That allowed her to be the expert not just on mining but on everything she read in the English language newspapers she accessed online every morning. So, when it came to writing about this United Nations assignment, I had only what she had told me. None of my old BHP contacts were aware of any assignments being conducted at the behest of the United Nations during Rebecca's time in the Resource Division. Nor could they remember her talking about her experiences in Pakistan or Kashmir before she joined the Resource Division, which led to the conclusion that no such assignment had taken place before she joined BHP, because Hugh and the others would surely have remembered her talking about it during all the times she monopolised conversation in the office.

After much searching on the internet, I did discover that during the 1980s, the United Nations Development

Program had been providing money and technical advice to the Pakistan Gemstone Corporation, which had been formed towards the end of the 1970s to commercialise the mining of gemstones in the region. According to a number of papers I was able to find, the intent was to provide the Pakistani government with the expertise to exert control over the extraction of precious stones, especially emeralds, from Kashmir and the Swat Valley, both of which had been mined using primitive methods for two millennia. The United Nations Development Program was assisting with funds and expert mining personnel to that end. Political unrest saw an end to United Nations involvement in the program, which collapsed in 1989. I can only assume that Rebecca had been a member of this expert panel between her exit from BHP and 1989, but I could find no details about the size of the panel, its makeup, where they went while in Pakistan and how long they were there.

I could not pinpoint exactly when Rebecca took this assignment to Kashmir, but I assume that it must have been soon after she left BHP, as it would have been difficult for her to have made such a trip once The Captain's health had deteriorated to the point at which taking extended leave away from Melbourne was impossible.

As well as the assignment in Pakistan she claimed to have done work in Papua New Guinea, although she provided no details about the nature of the work except that it involved the Papua New Guinea Bank and a company called Timim River Gold. She gave no indication that she actually visited the site. She could simply have read and commented on field reports sent to her by engineers and geologists on the ground. The same is true for the involvement she claimed to have had in an Austrade/Australian International Development Assistance Bureau mission to Burma in 1986. This project, undertaken jointly by the governments of Burma (now Myanmar) and Australia over the decade from 1977 to 1987, involved the installation of tube wells in a dry zone area of Myanmar and involved a number of Australian experts over the period. At the end of the project, a team of experts was sent by the Austrade/Australian International Development Assistance Bureau to examine the possibility of extending it and it is possible that Rebecca was part of this team.

From 1986, she was also providing advice on a regulations review being carried out by the Victorian Chamber of Mines in connection with the publication of the ANZMEC Safe Mining Handbook, which would later be adopted by all states in Australia. She also wrote a number of conference papers, including one presented to the AIDAB/WAIT Course of Third World Mining Officials in Perth in 1982, and another on Mine Dewatering which was presented at the Third International Mine Water Congress in Melbourne in 1988. According to some of the curriculum vitae, she was also engaged in a lengthy assignment with the Australian Securities Commission, but she gave no details about what this involved.

While Rebecca had mined all manner of minerals and precious stones over the years, it was her involvement in the extraction of dinosaur fossils on the rugged southern coast of Victoria at Cape Otway in 1989 that provided her with lasting satisfaction, so much so that they were a frequent topic of conversation over our afternoon drinks.

The chance discovery of fossil fragments by the renowned palaeontologist Tim Flannery a couple of decades earlier had sparked a search by a team of palaeontologists from the National Museum of Victoria (now Museums Victoria) for coastal rock outcrops which might yield more complete fossil samples. Led by Dr Tom Rich and his wife, Professor Pat Vickers-Rich, the search took them to an ancient stream channel at Cape Otway, but although the fossils they found were too water-worn to allow identification, the discovery indicated that there could be a major fossil deposit inside the vertical cliff face beyond the shore platform. It could only be accessed by tunnelling. With funds raised by the Friends of the National Museum of Victoria over the years and a team of willing but inexperienced volunteers, they began excavating the rock face at what became known as Dinosaur Cove, but progress was slow. Volunteers willing and able to use rock drills, sledgehammers and the like were in short supply, leading to a decision to seek an expert tunneller to tunnel into the cliff face.

Some initial work was done during the summer of 1988, with two roughly parallel tunnels and one connecting cross tunnel being cut into the cliff with the result that a tiny skull, later to be identified as a juvenile of a new species of hypsilophodontid, a small-bodied orthopod dinosaur, being found. It was named *Leaellynasaura amicagraphica* after the Richs' daughter Leaellyn. Rebecca was approached by the Inspector of Mines for Victoria on behalf of Dr Rich to extend the two parallel tunnels and cut another cross tunnel further inside the cliff. As luck would have it she was available, as The Captain was having one of his frequent spells in respite care.

Used to having a team of hard-working labourers she could order about on mine sites, her abrasive manner on the cliff face upset some of the crew assigned to drill holes for the explosives and to shovel up the debris after the charges had been fired. Most, if not all, had qualifications in palaeontology, geology and other earth sciences at least as respectable, if not better than her engineering degrees, and did not take kindly to being ordered about. They did, however, respect her ability, as one of the volunteers told the journalist from *National Geographic* who was on site to do a story on the dinosaurs, 'she was one tough woman. She was incredible. She used to carry sticks of gelignite between her boobs'.

Her unorthodox method of laying out a firing wall also came under criticism. Instead of drilling gelignite holes in a neat pattern, Rebecca took a random approach with no apparent order to the way in which the detonators were linked to each other. According to one of the team it looked like a madwoman's knitting, but it worked and the result was achieved. The team were able to find some more intact *Leaellynasaura amicagraphica* fossils for their collection and discover a distinctly different fossil of the same genus which they named after the Richs' son.

There was only one mishap during the time Rebecca was on site. She neglected on one occasion to clear the blasting chamber of a wheelbarrow before she fired the shot. It took off over the heads of the crew standing a safe distance away on the beach and landed in the cove. It was retrieved, in no worse shape than before it went into the water, except for a few more dents.

Her abrasiveness did come in handy after the camp had been set upon by a group of young lads who were holidaying nearby and thought they would have some sport vandalising the equipment on the beach. She caught them at it, chastised them sternly and then put them to work restoring the damaged items and helping the crew with rock clearing.

Although her work at Dinosaur Cove was finished once she had successfully extended the parallel tunnels and opened another cross tunnel exposing an area of rock in which the team hoped to find more complete fossils, her involvement continued for a couple of weeks after she had returned home to The Captain. On the evening of Australia Day, 1989, she got a frantic call for help from Tom Rich – the Panther Rock Drill was broken and none of the suppliers were contactable over the holiday weekend. She told him to bring it to her, greeting him at about midnight at the Toorak Road apartment dressed in a long black nightdress and smoking a cigarette in a holder which Tom claimed was at least twenty centimetres long. She spread out layers of newspaper on the carpeted floor and proceeded to give instructions for the dismantling of the greasy rock drill and its correct reassembly while walking back and forth, tapping her cigarette holder from time to time to dislodge a bit of ash. By 2 am the Panther Rock Drill was back together and Tom was sent on his way. He was not to know that she could not have come to him to repair the drill as by then The Captain was back in her care and asleep in his bedroom.

Life after the Captain

Around August 1989, Rebecca changed her business address to Canberra Road, South Yarra. This property, which The Captain had owned for many years, had until then been tenanted. Although two storeyed and divided into two apartments, the plan had apparently been to provide a more accessible space for the Department of Veterans Affairs' drivers and ambulance officers who called on a regular basis to transport The Captain to and from the repatriation services. To this end, she had part of the ground floor converted into a bedroom for the old man, using the rest of the space to expand her Norton Mining Services office. Unfortunately, The Captain did not live to experience his new surroundings, dying one month later on 10th September 1989.

Within a few months of the move, the unit in Toorak Road and the house in Canberra Road both came to Rebecca. In the copy of the will I obtained from the Public Records Office she was named as the Executor and Trustee of the will The Captain had written on the 23rd of May 1985. Apart from his 1954 Zephyr Convertible Sedan, which he left to his friend Dr Watson, and a handful of bequests to Jewish schools, synagogues and the

Montefiore Homes for the Aged, as well as to the Salvation Army and the Queen Victoria Medical Centre, the bulk of his property was left to Rebecca. He outlined his bequest to her as follows:

> To my said friend Rebecca Michelle Norton my properties now situate and known as (…) Canberra Road Toorak and (…) Toorak Road South Yarra together with all my furniture and furnishings and articles of personal and household use or ornament owned by me at the date of my death and the sum of FIVE THOUSAND DOLLARS ($5000.00)

Before probate could be applied for, however, a caveat had been placed on the will by Marion McCullock Nelken of Barkly St, Footscray, who claimed to have been the wife of The Captain and as such was entitled to a share in the property.

I had never heard any mention of the possibility that The Captain had been married in any of my conversations with Rebecca, but according to the Births, Deaths and Marriages website he had indeed been married in 1953 to Marion McCullock Lindsay. On TROVE I found further references in the digitised copies of *The Age* published during the 1950s to Mrs F.A. Nelken who, like her sister-in-law, the wife of The Captain's brother Louis, was involved in several charities such as the Robin Hood committee of the Helping Hand Association for mentally retarded children. She also accompanied her husband to functions, mostly hosted by Louis Nelken, around the same time. I could find no evidence of a divorce. On the 15th November 1989, she withdrew the caveat and nine days later probate was granted to Rebecca. The total value of The Captain's estate was calculated to be $1,155.992.

According to the valuations carried out on the Captain's estate, the Canberra Road property was worth $875,000 in 1989 and the Toorak Rd Apartment was $245,000. On top of that there were household effects of $35,850, a list of which, stretching over two pages, was attached to the will. It would seem that over the years The Captain had acquired some very expensive pieces of furniture including a 19th century Colonial sideboard valued at $6,000. Presumably it was sold, along with all the other items of furniture, glassware and ornaments as soon as they came into Rebecca's possession, because there was no sign of them in the Canberra Rd property when I visited her there some time in 1990 or 1991.

By then she had already sold both properties. According to the documents from Landata – Land Use Victoria, on the 5th February 1990 she sold the Toorak Rd property for $245,000, and by November 1990 she had also sold the Canberra Rd property for only $371,000. It seems that she came to an arrangement with the purchasers to continue occupying one of the two apartments into which it had been divided. Hence when I visited, she was still living there but did not own it.

She seemed to be well settled, though, with plenty of work to keep her busy judging by the piles of maps, charts and other material strewn across her work table. She had also acquired two dogs, the sharp-eyed part dingo Amber and a big timid Italian sheep dog called Tabatha. Neither were puppies, but where they came from I never did find out. While she obviously had come to an arrangement with the new owners of her apartment, the dogs were to present a problem for her whenever she was forced to move from then on.

It would appear that much of the work she was doing at the time could be completed in the comfort of her own office without the need for her to travel to mine sites and other areas under contention. Once she had received the surveys, assays, photographs and other technical data about a situation on which she had been asked to provide her expert opinion, she could ask for additional data to be sent to her and write a report. Occasionally she did have to present her report in person, as she did in a case concerning a proposal to allow gold fossicking within the township of Maryborough in Victoria, which concerned the Minister for Planning and Urban Growth in 1990 and was the subject of a hearing that stretched over several days at the courthouse in Maryborough. The proposal to allow fossicking within the township was denied on her advice that 'only competent major mining companies should work the alluvial deposits because they will contribute to the knowledge of the geology of the area ...'

According to one of Rebecca's curriculum vitae, she was often called on to join similar panels of experts to assess the viability or otherwise of prospective mines, such as a gold project in Tarnagulla, for which she was engaged to write a report. I was given a copy of the prospectus containing her report by one member of the old miners' grapevine, who was the principal member of the advisory panel. On this occasion her assessment of the viability concurred with the other experts, but situations did arise where there was no consensus, leading to the possibility that the experts themselves could find themselves challenged in court.

One such occasion arose when Rebecca was asked to give an opinion in a case involving a hostile takeover of a small gold mining company near Bendigo by one of the big players in the industry. On her advice, a complaint was made to the Australian Securities Commission that the share price of the predator company had been inflated, to the detriment of the shareholders of the small company. Charges were subsequently laid against the high-profile owner of the takeover company who, having been apprised of the fact that the complainants were acting on the advice of Rebecca Norton, was heard by several of her colleagues to make threats to destroy her financially.

The case went to court towards the end of 1994, with notice that there would be twenty-four witnesses called, although their names were not listed. After the first three had given their evidence, the ASC abruptly withdrew its complaint against the high-profile businessman and the remainder of the witnesses were dismissed. Although I spent hours searching the newspapers of the time to see if Rebecca's name was mentioned in relation to the case, I can only presume that she didn't get her day in court. Nor could I find any evidence that the magnate at the centre of this affair carried out his threat to destroy her, either through the courts or elsewhere. What I did discover was that, despite the inheritance Rebecca had received a few years earlier she was, by the time the ASC had abandoned the case, in dire financial straits. I was not able to access banking records, but judging from the annual returns she lodged for the first few years in which Norton Mining

Services was her main source of income, she was not earning enough to repay loans she had taken out. By the time she received the Captain's money she had a debt of $116,000.

Despite all the turmoil in her life, she threw herself enthusiastically into the activities of AUSIMM and MICA, organising activities, giving talks and writing papers to be presented at conferences. From 1991 she was a member of the VALMIN Committee, a joint committee of the Australasian Institute of Mining and Metallurgy and the Australian Institute of Geoscientists, which was established to develop and maintain the Australasian Code for public reporting of technical assessments and valuations of mineral assets. Prior to the publication of the VALMIN Code in 1995, MICA organised the Mineral Valuation Methodologies Conference, held in Sydney on 27 and 28 October 1994. According to one of the organisers who worked alongside Rebecca in the development of the Code and its presentation at the Conference, it was one of the best conferences ever held.

Costerfield

By 1995 I had left the picture-framing industry behind me and had taken a live-in job as a boarding house mistress at one of the posh Sydney girls' schools so that I had time to resume my academic studies. I could also enjoy the freedom the school holidays gave me to visit Margie and Barney in Melbourne. When I drove down during the winter term break in 1995, Margie told me that Rebecca was no longer living at the Canberra Road house, having sold it and bought a smaller and more convenient house in South Melbourne. She was obviously not aware that both the properties the Captain had left Rebecca in his will had long since been sold, and that she had only been renting the Canberra Road apartment. I decided not to enlighten her with the facts at the time, but I did get the address and telephone number from her and arrange to visit Rebecca.

Her new home was a small, single-storey terrace in poor condition in South Melbourne. I saw little of the interior except the kitchen and sitting room area, the only couches in which were occupied by the two dogs, who seemed unwilling to give up any of their comfort so I could sit down. There was no obvious sign of any Norton Mining Services activity, but she may have had an office set up in one of the two rooms off the passageway leading to the kitchen. I remember we went for a walk with the dogs and I bought her a sandwich, and she chatted along the way about the VALMIN project and other things before we returned to her place for a cup of weak tea.

During that year Emma had completed her term as Armaments Officer for the No 3 Squadron at the Williamstown Air Force Base and had transferred to Logistics Command in St Kilda Road. While she found suitable accommodation in Melbourne she stayed with her grandparents in Box Hill, and it was through her grandmother that she received an invitation to attend a birthday party in Rebecca's honour that December.

The party was arranged and catered for by a woman called Mary, who seemed to have befriended Rebecca, but I was never able to discover Mary's surname or where they had met. I did find out that Mary had been a milliner before taking a job as live-in housekeeper for a man called Geoffrey, who was in the late stages of multiple sclerosis.

Geoffrey was the son of a prominent Melbourne businessman and had been a journalist for many years until his illness forced him to retire. He lived in a big house in East Melbourne which had been adapted to his needs. The party Mary threw for Rebecca was held in its extensive garden. There were other guests including Hugh Mackinnon, who would become a valued informant when I began writing Rebecca's biography. Emma did find out that Rebecca was spending several hours each week reading the daily newspapers to Geoffrey, who was losing his sight. There was apparently an informal system of payment, supervised by his brother's business, for the handful of readers who had been assembled by Mary to provide an almost around the clock reading service.

Not long after this party, Margie told me that Rebecca was managing a mine at Costerfield in Central Victoria. She wasn't the Mine Manager – that position had already been filled by the mine owners, Australian Gold Development, who were in the process of re-opening a mine site that had operated on and off since 1860, following the discovery of gold there by two prospectors called Coster and Field. High levels of antimony which, for most of the next 100 years was seen as an almost worthless contaminant, had seen the original mine closed in 1883 and all subsequent attempts to make it viable short lived.

In 1993, Australian Gold Development NL took over the site with the intention of establishing a *carbon in pulp* process to separate the gold from the antimony in the tailings produced from previous mining ventures. They also had plans to develop a new open cut mine on the same site. For both operations to go ahead, the company was obliged to employ a mining engineer with a Mine Manager's ticket and Rebecca was available.

For her this must have been a dream come true. She was back to working where she was happiest, on site surrounded by mine workers she could order around while she supervised the construction of the *carbon in pulp* plant and oversaw open cut operations. She brought the two dogs up to Costerfield and moved into the Mine Manager's residence along with a female geologist called Grazyna, whose other name I have not been able to establish, so I was unable to track her down to ask about her time living and working with Rebecca. It seems, though, from the way Rebecca talked about her, that a great friendship developed between them that was only broken when the decision was made two years after the mine opened that neither the open cut nor the *carbon in pulp* plant operation were likely to meet the expectations of the Board of Australian Gold Development. The geologist moved on and Rebecca and her two dogs were suddenly left with no roof over their heads. She moved to Ballarat, giving Margie her telephone number and address, which she passed on to me.

Initially she had the best part of two years' salary in her bank account and was able to rent a fairly respectable three-bedroom home in the Ballarat suburb of Newington for herself and her dogs. She contacted the Ballarat University branch of MICA and renewed her involvement with AUSIMM while she sent off copies of her curriculum vitae in the hope of attracting work, all seemingly to no avail. By the time I saw her again, she was suffering from a level of despondency from which she would never really recover.

Broke in Ballarat

Margie must have picked up on Rebecca's despondency when they talked on the phone shortly after she had left Costerfield, but there was no possibility that Barney could drive her up to Ballarat. While he was valiantly trying to keep secret the fact that he had macular degeneration and was relying on Margie to tell him where the lines on the road and approaching traffic were, it was clear that he shouldn't be driving at all. But he wouldn't contemplate handing in his licence and Margie was not pressing him to do so, as that would put an end to trips to the shops and church on Sundays.

It was Emma who brought the issue to a head after he continued to drive around Box Hill like this despite pleas from other members of the family that he should stop. She offered to advertise the little blue Escort for sale and to vet potential buyers. Out of the replies to the advertisement she posted, she selected a young man who really needed a car for his work and was sensible enough to take loving care of it. Barney was satisfied and was happy to settle for the half price taxi service for which he and Margie were both eligible, but Margie still wanted to check on Rebecca.

I had been planning a trip to Ballarat the next time I was in Victoria because I had been offered a place at

Sydney University to do my PhD. I had already decided that my dissertation would comprise a work of fiction around Irish immigration to goldrush Ballarat, together with an exegesis which would explain my reason for the nature of my presentation and the history on which both the novel and the exegesis were based. Having one work of historical fiction about to be published and another on the way, both dealing with the plight of the Irish under British rule, I was keen to explore the conditions they experienced in goldrush Ballarat, where my own ancestors had settled.

When I contacted the University of Ballarat, now Federation University, to see if I could use their research facilities during the school holidays, I was offered a scholarship to complete my studies there on a part-time basis while continuing to live and work in Sydney. When I came down to meet the Head of the Humanities Department, I stayed a night with Rebecca.

It wasn't a pleasant experience. She talked incessantly about the Costerfield mine, her right-wing view of world politics and a host of other topics while preparing a meal in a kitchen full of unwashed dishes. She then made up a bed for me on the lounge room floor from cushions and rugs while she and the dogs shared a double bed. As there was no sign that she had any work as a consultant, I offered to pay her to do some research for me. I wanted to develop a picture of what life was like for the Catholic Irish in a city in which the Protestant majority despised them and the Catholic Church controlled the way they lived and raised their children. I chose to concentrate my research on the 1870s, because Catholics had been excluded by their clergy from attending the new free, compulsory, and secular schools which had been introduced throughout the colony of Victoria following the passing of the *Education Act*.

At this time the National Library program to digitise the major newspapers across the country was yet to start, but the Ballarat Mechanics' Institute had complete sets in hard copy of all the newspapers which had been circulated in Ballarat since the middle of the 1850s, so I joined myself and Rebecca up to access them. I explained what I was looking for and provided her with some parameters to guide her search and went back to Sydney to work. I expected her to give me a list of articles I could easily find when I returned to Ballarat during the next school holidays. Instead, she emailed me a page of quirky comments about things that had taken her fancy in the newspapers, but none of them were related to the topics I had asked her to look for. I gathered later from the Mechanics Institute staff that she spent a good deal of time in the Reading Room holding forth on her mining experiences to anyone who happened to be there at the time.

In October 1997, Jan died from a massive heart attack while she was being moved from the small bush hospital at Bruce Rock to a larger one at Merredin. I presume that Margie rang Rebecca to tell her of Jan's passing, but she almost certainly told her not to attend the funeral, as Auntie Noreen, Margie's youngest sister, who was a long-time resident of Western Australia, was expected to come up from Perth for the occasion. Liz and Louise flew from Melbourne with Margie and Barney, and I flew from

Sydney with my younger son, Phill, who was about to start work with a fishing company based in Fremantle. Rebecca's name was not mentioned in any of our conversations over the few days we were together.

As I had not seen Rebecca since that visit to Ballarat earlier in the year, I was unaware that her financial welfare and her mental and physical health were reaching a crisis point. I had not been back in Sydney long when I received an email from her informing me that she had had enough and was going to end it all. With thirty teenage girls in my care and no replacement on whom I could call I could not leave the school, so I rang the Salvation Army in Ballarat. The officer I talked to understood my predicament and offered to visit immediately. An hour later he rang to assure me that she was in no immediate danger of suicide because she still had the dogs with her. In his experience, he told me, people do not abandon their animals.

Apparently, Rebecca had been in possession of a number of credit cards on which she had been living since she finished working at Costerfield, and she had been playing one against the other until they were all maxed out. The man from the Salvos provided her with food for both her and the dogs, and arranged for the woman from their centre who dealt with financial situations such as Rebecca's to visit her. Within a few days, she had filed for bankruptcy and lodged an application for unemployment benefits. Rebecca didn't contact me again, but I was kept informed about what was happening. Thank God for the Salvos.

I took the summer school holidays to go to Ireland to do some more research for my thesis, assuming that now

Rebecca had a regular income and rent assistance from the Newstart allowance, all would be well. How wrong could I be? One Friday morning a month or so after I got back from Ireland and was again working at Abbotsleigh School, I got a call from Barney. Now Barney never used the phone – that was Margie's job, so I knew immediately that something was wrong. It seems that late the previous evening, without any notice, Rebecca arrived at their house in Box Hill in a pick-up truck along with all her belongings, minus the dogs, who had been surrendered to the pound. She and the driver of the truck proceeded to unpack her furniture, filing cabinets and clothes onto Barney's back lawn. Margie immediately went into a panic. What would the neighbours think? Then she developed such severe chest pains that Barney had to take her to Box Hill Hospital.

Fortunately, I had Fridays off and the university students who lived in the boarding house, and were rostered on for the weekend, were able to take over from me. I bought the first flight I could get to Melbourne and rang Emma, who was working in Melbourne, asking her to meet me and drive me out to Box Hill. By the time I got there, Margie had been discharged from the hospital, but Rebecca was not there. She told Barney that she had a job interview in the city, a condition of her Newstart allowance being that she actively search for work each fortnight.

Emma and I spent the evening searching the Real Estate section of the local papers to find accommodation that we thought Rebecca would be able to afford, eventually narrowing our search area to Melbourne's inner west, which was where we headed the next morning. It took us most of the day, but eventually we found a one-bedroom unit in Spotswood in reasonable condition that was available immediately. There was no possibility that the agent would consider Rebecca as a tenant, so I filled out the rental application in my name and offered to pay the bond on the spot. By the time we got back to Emma's place in Footscray, my application had been approved. The next day we went to the shops to purchase new bedding, kitchen necessities and food so that she could move in first thing Monday morning.

I spoke to Barney, who knew a man who knew a man with a small van who could come early on Monday to bring Rebecca and all her belongings to Spotswood. Once they were safely inside the unit I went to Williamstown, so that we could notify Centrelink of her change of address. I also arranged for her to have the telephone connected and her account with Telstra reinstated. I then bought her a meal before dropping her back at her new home. I was booked on an evening flight to Sydney.

It was while we were waiting to be attended to at Centrelink that I became aware that, rather than being thankful for what the Salvos had done for her, she was angry, firstly for arranging for her to receive unemployment benefits and then for assisting her to file for bankruptcy. There was a touch of Margie's snobbery about her attitude. I could almost imagine her saying: 'Our family does not file for bankruptcy!'

She also resented the fact that the age at which women could apply for the Age Pension was about to be increased from 60 to 62, making her ineligible for another couple of years, and she was firmly of the opinion that the commitments Centrelink imposed on those receiving unemployment benefits were unjust. When I was searching through the handful of files that remained after her death, I found a letter she had written to an Inquiry into Older Unemployed People conducted by the Federal Government the following year. It was a couple of pages long. Below are a few extracts:

> ... I have been registered with Centrelink and receiving benefits for 20 months. Each week I apply for several positions and I am not proud. I do not need to advise you what Mining Engineering is like at the moment even with a Mine Managers Certificate and an impressive cv. The Industry and its professions are actually quite small so there is little about me that is not known.
>
> ... I am type cast even by people who should know better. Part of that type casting is that I am only what I am qualified in ... I have acquired many job skills but some that once needed no ticket now do, or at least that is a nice way of filtering me out.
>
> ... Centrelink referred me to 'Intensive Assistance.' It was neither. I was already doing the one relevant suggestion made, ie., removing the heroic and the high-profile positions in industry and the Professional Associations from my cv as well as deleting anything that could be used to guess my age.
>
> ... If people like me are to be lepers to family and profession we may need a colony. There are some quite liveable places where we could be out of sight and stop cluttering up the recruiting agents mail. And at least the social researchers would know where to find us.

The letter included several other pieces of advice for Centrelink as to how they could better deal with the unemployed, especially those like her who were much better educated and experienced than the crop of Centrelink employees with whom she had to deal. It does not appear that she received any notification of receipt of her letter, much less a reply.

Coming Home

By the time my PhD candidature was confirmed in September 1998, I had decided that studying part-time for such an important qualification was too difficult. Besides, I had had enough of living in a school boarding house with 30 Year Nine girls. I was able to change my status and scholarship to full time with Ballarat University, so at the beginning of 1999 I packed my belongings into my little car and drove down to Victoria, renting a small unit in Buninyong until I could move into the house in Eureka Street on which I had taken out a mortgage the year before, using some superannuation money I had from a previous job. After living so far distant from family for so long, it was a pleasure to be able to visit Margie and Barney and Rebecca much more regularly.

I was pleased to find that Rebecca had begun reading newspapers again to her friend Geoffrey, whose multiple sclerosis had deteriorated to such an extent that he could no longer be cared for at home and had been moved by his family into a private nursing home in East Melbourne, run by the religious sisters who staffed St. Vincent's Hospital. The reading roster, Rebecca told me, was now being managed by Geoffrey's sister-in-law, who also looked after the amount of remuneration being paid to each reader. It was a relief to know that Rebecca had a small source of income, which she had not declared to Centrelink, so that it did not impact on her pension.

I would telephone Rebecca before I left Ballarat and would arrive in Spotswood to find her sitting on the low brick fence in front of her block of units. If she was not rostered on to read for Geoffrey that day, we would go to Williamstown for lunch and I would stop off at the little grocery shop near her place on the way back so she could buy a couple of bottles of Cockatoo Ridge sparkling wine. I presumed at the time that they were her weekly supply, but I was very wrong, as I found out a couple of years later.

If she was rostered on to read for Geoffrey when I arrived, I drove her into the nursing home in East Melbourne, where she assured me that she would be provided with a meal by the nursing home staff, and headed out to Box Hill to see Margie and Barney. After the obligatory cup of milky tea, I would ask them if they wanted to go anywhere. Invariably, Barney wanted to go to Bunnings, so he could join the small legion of little old men who wandered up and down the aisles fingering the tools on display and picking up small packets of nails, screws and drill bits while they imagined what they would use them for it they still could. While I was waiting for him to return to the car, I often wondered if the Bunnings management realised what a service they were providing to the elderly men of Australia who could still dream of being useful and needed in their communities. Fortunately, Bunnings in Nunawading, which was the closest store to Box Hill, had a small café where Margie could sit and drink coffee while we waited. When I was helping to pack up the unit to which Margie and Barney had moved. once Barney could no longer drive, I came across all these unopened packets of screws and nails, enough to last me forever.

Barney died on January 18 2000 from complications due to heart surgery which he probably didn't need. He had had a heart murmur for most of his life but had been persuaded that his health would be better if he had a valve replaced. He was already 85 years old, and while the operation was carried out successfully, he succumbed to Golden Staph while in hospital and then to Guillain-Barré syndrome, which at his age proved fatal. Despite her grief at losing her soulmate of 60 years, Margie still had family appearances to consider. I was sent to inform Rebecca of Barney's death, with advice that she was not welcome at the Requiem Mass in Box Hill. It was one of the hardest things I ever had to do, and Rebecca was visibly hurt, but she agreed to stay away for Margie's sake. Once again, we were given a story for the relatives should they ask, 'Where's Rob?' but nobody did. They all knew.

Not long after I returned to Ballarat, I had coffee with one of my Norton cousins who, as soon as we took our table in the coffee shop said, 'Tell me about Rob!' So, I did – the gender change, Rebecca's adopted name, her exclusion from the family and where she was currently living. My cousin was surprised and perhaps a little shocked, but she was more annoyed by her Auntie Margie's lies and evasiveness. The next time I saw her she told me that she had visited Auntie Sheila, Barney's younger sister, who was still living independently in Ballarat and told her all about Rebecca. She was surprised by Sheila's response. She said:

'Thank goodness! So that's all that happened. I thought Rob must have been mixed up in drugs and was languishing in some Thai jail with Gary Glitter.' The British rock singer, whose real name was Paul Gadd, had been in the news at the time, having been jailed for child sex offences.

Auntie Sheila, of course, told Barney's older sister Marie, who was also living in Ballarat, and between them the story of Rebecca's gender change spread throughout the Norton family. A few years after Marie and Sheila had followed Barney to the grave, Marie's son John decided that the remaining Norton cousins should come together, so he organised a Cousins Day for us at his home at Ocean Grove. I made Rebecca a new outfit for the occasion – a jacket over a blouse and a wraparound skirt, the sort she liked but with more material in it than the one she usually wore, which was in the habit of parting to show too much when she sat down. Of course, she carried a shopping bag, as she did wherever she went, and she wore a wide brimmed hat that had seen better days and she was obviously nervous as we drove down to his house. There was an audible pause from all the cousins assembled on the patio of John's house as we walked in, but then someone put a beer into Rebecca's hand and mentioned the YCW Harriers and the tension lifted. Most of the male members of the family had at one time run for the Harriers and a few of the girls had married Harriers men, so there was plenty to talk about.

It turned out to be a great day for all of us. We talked about our children and, for those who had them, grandchildren. We flashed photos around and exchanged addresses and telephone numbers and generally caught up with what everyone had been doing since we last met. I doubt that Rebecca ate any of the buffet that John and Nan had prepared, nor did she drink very much – she was too busy reminiscing. She was exhausted by the time we left for the drive back to Ballarat, but she was also the happiest I had seen her. I will be forever grateful to John for giving her back the family she thought she had lost long since.

Rescuing Rebecca from Herself

I continued driving down to Melbourne once a week after Barney died, because Margie needed me more than ever. During their sixty years of marriage, Barney had always treated her as his delicate princess, doing all the heavy jobs around the house like the vacuum cleaning and the washing. She had no idea how to use the washing machine they had had for ages. It was a pretty ordinary little machine, but she was reluctant to learn, despite me simplifying the instructions as much as I could.

While she could easily catch a bus to the Box Hill Shopping Centre from just outside her house, and she did have a half-price taxi card, she preferred to wait until I could take her there. She wanted me to follow the pattern she and Barney had set – coffee and cake at their favourite café followed by a wander around the mall before she picked up whatever she needed at the supermarket. If I had already taken Rebecca to Geoffrey's nursing home, she knew she had me for the rest of the day, so she would often have a list of other chores she needed me to attend to before I headed back to Ballarat.

It had been my habit to telephone both Margie and Rebecca before I left Ballarat, so they would both be waiting for me when I arrived. On Boxing Day, 2021 I got no answer to my call to Rebecca but I came anyway, expecting to find her waiting, but there was no sign of her so I went to her door. I knocked for quite a while before she opened it just a crack. She looked dishevelled, hair undone and a none too clean dress hanging from her shoulders. I had noticed over previous visits that she appeared to have lost weight, but she had assured me that she was eating well so I didn't push the issue.

I put my foot in the door to prevent her from shutting it, but she blocked me with her body from seeing inside. For a while we stood facing each other, at an impasse, but eventually I got her to admit that the apartment was in such a mess that she couldn't stand living in it. She told me that when she was not at the nursing home in East Melbourne reading to Geoffrey, she was living on Spotswood Station. There was a pie shop nearby where she could buy a pie for lunch, the only meal she was having each day.

Knowing that she would probably be able to share Geoffrey's lunch at the nursing home, I persuaded her to get dressed so I could drive her to East Melbourne. I told her that I would clean up the apartment and fetch her at the end of the day, but at that stage I didn't know how big a job it was going to be. Once I got the front door open wide enough for me to squeeze through, I knew. There was not an inch of floor that was not covered by old furniture and rubbish. Stopping the door from opening fully was an old broken wooden wardrobe which had not been part of the belongings she had brought from Ballarat. There were several old computers, one sitting on a desk and the others on the floor, but it didn't seem that any were working. Most were not even connected. I can only presume that she had picked them out of someone else's hard rubbish.

The biggest problem was the fridge. It had been pulled out from the wall and was partially blocking access to the little kitchen. I opened the door, but shut it just as quickly. It had not been working for some time, but still had food in it, which was putrid. The sink was full of unwashed dishes and there were the remains of meals on the benches which appeared to have been there for some time. In amongst them were unopened bills and letters from Centrelink. I gathered them up, hoping against hope that the pile didn't include an eviction notice.

Knowing that the task was beyond me, I rang my son Phill, who was taking a holiday with friends in Melbourne before returning to his fishing trawler. He came straight away. While I was waiting for him I found a skip operator who was answering his phone, despite it being a public holiday, and asked him to deliver a skip as soon as he could. He was there within an hour and we began filling it. Phill prised open one of the doors to the wardrobe to find it stacked to the top with empty bottles of Cockatoo Ridge bubbly. We started counting them as we carried them out. Between the ones in the wardrobe and the others that were filling kitchen cupboards we think we reached a thousand.

Based on the promise I planned to make to Rebecca that I would find her a working computer, those on the floor and the desk went into the skip on top of the bottles. The old wardrobe went on top of them, clearing enough space for Phill to drag the fridge out. I had warned him not to open it, so we sat it beside the skip in the hope that the skip operator would take it with him when he came back a few days later.

I only had time to wash some of the dishes before I had to go back to East Melbourne for Rebecca. On the way back to Spotswood, I bought her some dinner and told her what I had done. She was neither grateful nor resentful – she seemed beyond caring. I promised I would be down from Ballarat early the next morning to take her back to East Melbourne so Phill and I could get on with the cleaning.

The next morning, I arrived with mops, brooms and cleaning products to continue the work once I returned from driving Rebecca into East Melbourne. While I waited for Phill to arrive, I decided to attack the bedroom. The bed and all the space around it were stacked high with newspapers, which I began pulling out and depositing in the skip. Only when Phill and I had most of them out did we discover that most of the mattress was also missing. It had been burnt down to the springs, and the base on which it had been sitting was a charred ruin. As I didn't have the money to replace it myself, I rang Margie, explaining the state in which Rebecca had been living and my fear that unless I got the apartment cleaned up and liveable, she would once again be homeless. As the memory of Rebecca lobbing in on her and Barney in Box Hill was still vivid, she was only too happy to provide money for a new bed for her. I left Phill removing the rest of the rubbish from the apartment while I went to one of the bargain furniture shops in Footscray.

Emma had been unable to lend a hand with the cleaning as she was busy showing an Italian she had met in a language school in Venice the highlights of Victoria, but she did give me her fridge. She had been planning to buy herself a larger one anyway. Once the Italian had gone on his way the following week, she went shopping for bedlinen, curtains, new saucepans and a nice little table and chairs. We spent the first Saturday of the new year scrubbing carpets and walls so that by the time the new bed was delivered, the apartment was clean enough to pass any rental inspection. While I fetched Rebecca from East Melbourne, Emma went to the grocery shop to restock the fridge. She bought a couple of bottles of Cockatoo Ridge to make the place more welcoming.

Over the next couple of weeks, I sorted out the problem with the phone and had it reconnected, and I made sure that on the day I visited her she had a substantial meal in Williamstown before I went on to visit Margie. In the meantime, I prepared simple meals like pasties, bolognaise and casseroles that I froze and took down for her. Whether she ate them or not I don't know, but she did seem to gain a little weight as the year progressed.

All Together in Ballarat

By 2004, my doctorate had been conferred and I had been commissioned to write the history of Catholic Education in the Diocese of Ballarat. This was a huge task, as the diocese covered the whole of the western half of Victoria, stretching from Mildura in the north to the Great Ocean Road in the south, with Ballarat and its satellite parishes making up its eastern boundary. There was a deadline on the project which meant that I needed to limit the amount of time I could give to being a taxi driver in Melbourne for Margie and Rebecca.

It was around this time that I heard that the Sisters of Nazareth, whose orphanages had been part of Ballarat Catholic history since the 1880s, had been undertaking major renovations to their large red brick building on the shore of Lake Wendouree. As the policies towards the care of vulnerable children had undergone considerable changes in recent times, the need for the kind of orphanages the sisters had run had steadily diminished, prompting them to turn their attention towards another need, that of aged care. Their buildings, however, needed major renovation to meet modern standards. Included in the renovations were a small number of self-contained independent living units suitable for people like Margie, who was well able to care for herself but needed the company of others in a friendly environment. After a fair amount of persuasion, she agreed to come up and inspect the units for herself. Reassured that she would be able to join in or ignore the activities available to the residents of the nursing home part of the complex as she saw fit, she decided to put the Box Hill unit on the market and move to Ballarat as soon as it sold.

I still had to go to Melbourne to see Rebecca every week and drive her into Geoffrey's nursing home. By this time, she was his only reader, as he was very ill. I doubt that he heard much of what was being read to him, but he undoubtedly enjoyed her company. She fed him his meals while she was there and the nursing staff showed their appreciation of her efforts by ensuring that she had a midday meal, for which I was grateful, as the thought of her eating a pie on Spotswood station was still fresh in my memory. By this time, she was getting the Aged Pension, so her requirement to find other work was gone and she had the additional money Geoffrey's family continued to pay for her services.

When Geoffrey died in May 2005, I told Rebecca that I thought it was time she moved to Ballarat. She was surprisingly receptive to the idea given the cloud under which she had departed the city in 1998. The move was not as traumatic as the previous one, nor was the clean-up afterwards as difficult. She had made an effort to dispose of newspapers, empty champagne bottles and other rubbish on a regular basis, so that was not an issue. With Emma's help we packed her clothes and other belongings, minus the computer, which had been drowned in champagne, for the courier we hired to bring them to Ballarat, and we cleaned the walls and floor as well as we could. I had already decided that I would not try to get back the bond I had paid, assuming that the letting agent would employ a professional cleaner before re-letting the unit.

I had found a one-bedroom unit in Canadian, the suburb adjacent to Ballarat East where I was living, and paid the bond before bringing her up to Ballarat. She was thrilled with it. The units had been built some twenty or thirty years earlier by a Dutch builder who, now that he had retired, was a regular visitor to his property, doing odd jobs or simply pottering about. As Rebecca was the only one of the tenants who was regularly home during the day, he was always in for a chat with her.

Margie was none too happy about having to share Ballarat with Rebecca. She made it quite clear that they were never to be seen in the same place at the same time, so a chore like grocery shopping, which should have taken no more than an hour or so, occupied a whole day. Margie had to have tea and cake at one of the coffee shops in or around Bridge Mall before she had me push the trolley up and down the aisles in Coles, while she decided what she needed. She never stockpiled to save coming back the next week and never prepared a list. In the fruit and vegetable section she would wander about squeezing the fruit on display to ensure that it was ripe, but not too ripe, before choosing a couple of pieces.

By the time I got Margie back to her unit and unpacked her shopping it was nearly lunchtime, so I would take

Rebecca for coffee and a pie at the pie shop near Coles before she would start her shopping. Initially she could manage to push her trolley by herself, but as time went on and her health deteriorated, I would have to take over. She was still buying a carton of cigarettes with each shop. I would then take her to the big discount liquor shop while she bought whatever brand of cheap bubbly was on special that week. Because of her health, it was left to me to carry all her shopping up the steps into her apartment.

Every Sunday afternoon I took Margie for tea and scones, usually to one of the cafés in Ballarat or the surrounding districts. Every now and then she would ask to be taken further afield, usually to Beaufort or Creswick, and she would tell me that I could bring Rebecca, because she didn't know anyone who lived in those towns and presumed the people there didn't know her. Rebecca always came, but was clearly uncomfortable, which meant that I was left with keeping the dialogue going. Afterwards I drove back to Ballarat, dropping Rebecca off first before taking Margie to Nazareth House. On one occasion she took out her purse, opened it and produced a $50 note which she handed to me saying, 'Buy him a new petticoat. The one he is wearing is looking terrible.'

Soon after Rebecca was settled, I enrolled her in the Ballarat chapter of U3A, the University of the Third Age, that wonderful institute run by older Australians for their peers who are intent on keeping their minds and bodies active as they age. I had been teaching a class in Irish History for some time, so I thought there would be a class Rebecca could enjoy. She chose Latin – everything she had learnt from the Christian Brothers was still tucked away in her photographic memory, and she was soon blitzing the class with her knowledge.

To keep her actively involved in the world, and to avoid the necessity for her to walk as far as Bridge Mall in all weathers to buy newspapers, we bought another cheap laptop and Emma installed a program called Paperboy, which allowed her to access English language newspapers across the world. To accommodate them all she began rising at 4am, making a coffee to have with the first cigarette of the day and then delving into the major news coming out in English from countries as far afield as Britain, the Middle East, South East Asia, Japan and China. By 4pm she was reading the *Toronto Globe and Mail*.

About that time each day I had set aside whatever research I was engaged in to walk my boxer dog, Maud. We usually reached Rebecca's unit at about 4.30pm and she was waiting for us. While she regurgitated the news of the day and her opinions on what political leaders of all stripes should be doing in their respective countries, she drank her cheap champagne, and I listened over a glass of the Irish whiskey I kept there for the purpose. She had favourites among the political leaders. From different sides of the spectrum she was particularly fond of Angela Merkel and Vladimir Putin and I think that in her mind she was advising them on how to run their respective countries. I wonder what she would tell Putin now.

Requiem

Margie died suddenly the day after New Year in 2012. She had not been unwell – in fact she had been extraordinarily well for a nearly 96-year-old at her cousin's funeral a few days previously, soaking up all the attention being given to her by extended family members from her father's side of the family who had come up from the Western District for the occasion. It was a surprise then when two sisters from Nazareth House rang to tell me that they were sending her over to the hospital in an ambulance. Within an hour, I had been informed that a valve at the top of her stomach had given way and that on someone so old, major surgery to repair it was impossible. I stayed by her bedside as she slipped into unconsciousness, while Emma began the process of notifying the family. As it was holiday time, reaching them was not easy, particularly my sister Louise, who had a senior position at the Australian High Commission in India, and none of them could get to Ballarat before Margie slipped away at about four the next morning.

When I saw Rebecca later that morning she immediately informed me that she wouldn't be going to the funeral. I remember saying, 'Of course you are going to the funeral!' But she shook her head and said, 'What about Uncle Jack?' Jack was married to Margie's sister, Tess, who was the only other member of the ten O'Farrell children still alive. Over the years he had adopted a patriarchal role at family gatherings, and while Rebecca had not seen him since her gender affirmation, she seemed to fear his disapproval. I told her, 'To hell with Uncle Jack. You are coming to the funeral.'

Arranging a Requiem Mass at St Alipius' Church in the week after New Year was not easy, but it had to be a Requiem and it had to be at St Alipius, for that was where Margie and Barney had been married. The few days we had to wait until the priest could accommodate us were a blessing, though, as it gave the more distant members of the family, including my sons, time to make their way to Ballarat.

When I met Phillip at the airport he was wearing a singlet, stubbies and thongs but he assured me that he had freshly ironed clothes in his backpack. I doubt they got very close to an iron, but I consoled myself that he would look no more scruffy than Rebecca, who I expected would be wearing the usual wrap-around skirt and big hat, but she surprised me. From out of one of those bags of clothes we had brought up from Spotswood she had dug out a very respectable navy skirt and jacket along with a pale blue blouse. She was wearing stockings and high-heeled shoes and her hair was neater than it had been in years.

She thoroughly enjoyed the funeral. The last Mass she had attended had been said in Latin and while she lamented the passing of a tradition, she enjoyed the ability of the congregation to participate in the service. She also enjoyed chatting to all the cousins and joining the smokers outside the church. As Margie was to be buried alongside Barney in the lawn section of the Necropolis in Springvale, I gave Rebecca time to say her goodbyes before I took her home. There had been more than enough excitement for one day.

I had arranged with the Necropolis for a new plaque to be made for Margie and Barney's grave and when it had been put in place Emma and I drove down to Springvale to check that the details were correct. As Uncle Jack and Auntie Tess lived in Springvale, we arranged to visit them as well. Over endless cups of tea and sandwiches we made small talk for ages before I told them that Rebecca was concerned that her appearance at Margie's funeral would have been a shock to them. They weren't shocked or surprised, but they were amused. They had known about Rebecca's gender change since the late 70s when she had gone to Western Australia in relation to the work she was doing for BHP – Noreen had told them, they said.

Noreen had been the youngest of Margie's siblings. She had met and fallen for a RAAF radio engineer called Ted who had been stationed in Ballarat after World War II, and had followed him to Western Australia when he was transferred there. Once he left the Air Force he worked in the mining industry. According to him, news of Rebecca's transformation spread like wildfire around the mining community and Noreen had passed on the details to Tess, but at no stage did she consider telling Margie they knew the real reason Rebecca was not at any family functions.

I was saved from exposing my annoyance with them by Emma, who suggested that we hit the road so as to be back in Ballarat before dark, but my fury didn't abate. I could not help thinking that Rebecca had needlessly been excluded from contact with her extended family because Margie had been desperately trying to keep a secret that was known to all of the O'Farrell side of the family.

Slow Decline

Rebecca was diagnosed with emphysema shortly after moving to Ballarat. That did not stop her smoking, as she considered the damage had already been done and she might as well enjoy the few pleasures she still had in life. The old Dutch landlord was complicit in this, as he allowed her to smoke inside her unit, except in the bedroom, which was a relief to me. The thought of her setting fire to another mattress while she was sleeping was too horrible to contemplate.

In 2010, the landlord decided that he had had enough of maintaining the units and put them on the market. The new buyer was not so lenient – after inspecting the units she made it quite clear that there was to be no smoking at all indoors. Rather than give up her daily routine, Rebecca was still lighting up at 4am before turning on her computer to read the newspapers, only now she had to stand on the little square of concrete at the top of the stairs to her front door. In Ballarat's winter, both the smoking and the cold had a detrimental effect on her emphysema and by Autumn 2012 she was having great difficulty breathing, particularly at night. She would ring me every few nights, gasping down the phone that she couldn't breathe, and I would go and pick her up and take her to the emergency department of Ballarat Hospital. Then I would sit there until her turn to be seen and she was taken into the emergency ward. Sometimes they would keep her overnight, but most times, having oxygenated her, they would discharge her around midnight with advice to see her own doctor.

This went on until the middle of the year and until she had worn out her welcome at the hospital. I was advised to find her a place in an aged care facility and given the name of a nursing home in Hepburn Springs. The next day I drove her to what seemed like a well-appointed facility and saw her into a nice ground floor unit with the promise to bring her computer, television and champagne the next day.

Before I could gather up her belongings the next morning, the matron of the facility was on the phone. Rebecca had been up gasping for air most of the night and there was nothing the night staff could do for her because none of them had nursing training. I abandoned loading the television into my car and drove back out to Hepburn Springs in pouring rain with no idea what I would do with Rebecca once I got there. I packed the few belongings she had with her into the car and headed back to Ballarat with the front left-hand window wide open and Rebecca hanging out of it.

Hepburn Springs is about a kilometre past Daylesford, which had its own hospital, admittedly old and mainly used for maternity patients, but it did have an infrequently used emergency department. Rather than continue all the way to Ballarat with rain coming in the open windows, I pulled in there and rang the emergency bell furiously. Eventually a nurse answered my call, took one look at Rebecca and admitted her. She was there for the next six weeks while they tried to stabilise her.

Daylesford hospital had a long term stay facility in Creswick to which she was moved while I found a permanent aged care facility that would take her. Easier said than done. She had no assets, she was a smoker and drinker. I applied to every facility in and around Ballarat, except Nazareth House, as I knew she would not want to live there. My condition was that they had to have a nurse on duty at all times.

Eventually, I found a place for her at Kirralee in Ballarat East. It wasn't the fanciest of nursing homes I visited, but it had everything Rebecca needed, including a designated smoking area in one of the courtyards. There she could sit for hours yarning to other old codgers who were smoking their way into oblivion. I organised for her favourite newspapers to be delivered and, with the management's permission, I used some of the money Margie had left us to buy a small fridge in which she could keep her champagne and chocolate coated ice creams cold. Emma bought a new laptop to replace the one we had bought for her when she moved to Ballarat – that too had been drowned in champagne a short time earlier.

At first, she was quite content. Her health initially improved due to the care of the staff, who saw to it that the right medication was taken at the right time. Her room was well-heated and the meals were better than those she had been preparing for herself. Inevitably though the emphysema worsened and the walk to the smoking area became too much for her. Again with the management's permission, I bought a red ride-on mobility scooter so she had more freedom to get around. She started joining in the Saturday morning quiz competition the occupational therapists ran each week, dazzling the other residents with her knowledge.

After a time though, I began to notice that the normally white walls of the passage that led to her bedroom had streaks of red on them at about the height of the wheel covers of the scooter. It wasn't long before there were restrictions imposed on its use by the nursing staff. She would be allowed to use it in the mornings provided she did not start drinking champagne until after lunch, at which time they would take the key. Although annoyed at losing some of her independence, she accepted the conditions for a while. Then one day I arrived to be confronted by a new crisis. She had run into another resident and the scooter had to go. It was the beginning of the downward spiral. Her mobility, limited as it was, had been further reduced. She could no longer reach the smoking area and smoking was not permitted in the bedrooms.

With the management's blessing I began investigating e-cigarettes, which were still relatively unknown at the time. I found a firm which supplied a product that I was assured contained no nicotine, which Rebecca was willing to try, but they presented more problems than they solved. She could not resist dismantling the charger and reassembling it, she lost parts and broke others, so I gave up. Around this time her doctor decided that her lung capacity had diminished to such a level that she needed to be on oxygen permanently, which meant that smoking of any kind was out of the question.

She compensated by starting to drink as soon as her breakfast tray was taken away. One day I arrived to find that she had consumed three bottles of bubbly the previous day and had been unmanageable by evening. We reached another compromise: I would continue to buy the champagne but it would be stored in the nurses' fridge. At three o'clock every day one of the staff would bring her a cold bottle. She had no choice but to agree, although she was far from happy.

She still had her newspapers and her computer, although it was being used less and less each day. Her political views had always been very right wing, and we had in the past left the subject alone. As her world was becoming smaller and smaller, she got satisfaction from baiting me with her opinions. She was a great fan of Tony Abbott when he was Prime Minister and would demand that I respect him. If I asked, 'Why?' her answer was always, 'He's one of us.' By that she meant that he was a Catholic, which amused me. After all, the last Mass she had heard before Margie's Requiem was in Latin.

Although her television was always on she rarely paid it much attention, except on the day the Royal Commission into the Institutional Abuse of Children came to Ballarat, when she searched the screen looking for Brother McCarthy, or when there was a story about George Pell's fall from grace. She hated him as much as she hated McCarthy.

As I had Rebecca's Power of Attorney and had been managing her affairs since before she came to Ballarat, I had a sheaf of papers ready for her inevitable passing. Whenever I was away from Ballarat, I gave these papers to Emma in case she had to act on my behalf. Invariably she would meet me at the airport and hand them back to me, but in August 2017 I was in Cornwall, having just completed a summer school at Oxford, so it was Emma whom Kiralee rang when the end came. After all the time that I had spent with Rebecca over the previous seventeen years, I was not there to say goodbye.

www.ingramcontent.com/pod-product-compliance
Lightning Source LLC
Chambersburg PA
CBHW042138160426
43200CB00020B/2973